BBC

GCSE BITESIZE revision

KT-495-585

English

Trevor Gamson, Imelda Pilgrim
and Marian Slee

Published by BBC Educational Publishing,
Woodlands, 80 Wood Lane, London W12 0TT

First published 2002

© Trevor Gamson, Imelda Pilgrim, Marian Slee/BBC Worldwide
(Educational Publishing), 2002

ISBN: 0 563 54457 0

Colour reproduction by Spectrum Colour, England

Printed and bound by Poligrafico Dehaniano, Italy

BBC

Contents

Non-fiction texts

Acknowledgements

Every effort has been made to trace the copyright holders of material used in this book. If, however, any omissions have been made, we would be happy to rectify this at the earliest opportunity.
'Action for Blind People' letter © Action for Blind People 2002; 'Albert Docks' courtesy of The Mersey Partnership; *Coping with parents* (cover and text) by Peter Corey, Scholastic Children's Books, 1989. Permission granted by Scholastic Children's Books; 'Easy pickings' and 'Alarms' articles courtesy of *Which? Magazine*; 'Gee, Mum' courtesy of *The Daily Mail*; 'How to vote' leaflet courtesy of Her Majesty's Stationery Office; 'In peak condition' courtesy of Health Education Authority; 'Is it fair to put Mum in a home?' article courtesy of *Woman Magazine*; 'Kaylee' reprinted courtesy of *The Mail on Sunday*; 'Meet Sundance' courtesy of the Whale and Dolphin Conservation Society; 'Ninja peril', 'Fireworks: time for a total ban?' and 'Quiet please' courtesy of *Manchester Evening News*; 'No time to draw breath?' courtesy of Macmillan Cancer Relief; 'North Cyprus' (advertisement) courtesy of North Cyprus Tourism Centre; 'Oxfam' (advertisement) reproduced by permission of Oxfam Publishing, 274 Banbury Road, Oxford, OX2 7DZ; 'Queen 71' 'Hitting out' and 'Hi-tech, low life' articles courtesy of Guardian Newspapers Ltd; 'Rhino adoption papers'. We thank WWF –UK for the permission to reproduce this text; 'RSPCA' (advertisement) courtesy of the RSPCA; 'She's old enough to look after her own smile' courtesy of Greater Mcr. East Education and Training Consortium; 'Toaster safeguards' courtesy of Kenwood Ltd; 'Wheels are a wonder' courtesy of Mountain Bike UK; 'Wild refuge' and 'How green are you?' courtesy of *BBC Vegetarian Good Food Magazine*.

Introduction

About Bitesize

GCSE Bitesize is a revision service designed to help you achieve success at GCSE. There are books, television programmes and a website, each of which provides a separate resource designed to help you get the best results.

TV programmes are available on video through your school, or you can find out transmission times by calling 08700 100 222.

The website can be found at http://www.bbc.co.uk/schools/gcsebitesize/

About this book

This book is your all-in-one revision companion for GCSE.
It gives you the three things you need for successful revision:

1 Every topic clearly organised and clearly explained
2 The most important facts and ideas highlighted for quick checking: in each topic and in the extra sections at the end of this book
3 All the practice you need: in the 'check' questions in the margins, in the practice sections at the end of each topic, and in the exam questions at the end of this book

Each topic is organised in the same way:

- **The bare bones** – a summary of the main points, an introduction to the topic, and a good way to check what you know

- **Key points** highlighted throughout

- **Check questions** in the margin – have you understood this bit?

- **Remember tips** in the margin – extra advice on this section of the topic

- **Exam tips** in red – specific things to bear in mind for the exam

- **Practice questions** at the end of each topic – a range of questions to check your understanding

The extra sections at the back of this book will help you to check your progress and be confident that you know your stuff.

Exam questions and model answers:

- A selection of exam questions with the model answers explained to help you get full marks

About this book continued

Complete the facts
- Another resource for you to use as you revise: fill in the gaps to complete the facts
- Answers in the answer section

Last-minute learner
- The most important facts in just two pages

Using this book

This BITESIZE book is divided into two main sections:

Literary texts

This contains four units on poetry, in which you will consider the meaning and structure of poems and how the poets use language to help get their meaning across to the reader. There is also a section on *Romeo and Juliet*, which you may be studying for coursework. This section deals with important ideas in the play and introduces you to a range of dramatic techniques.

Non-fiction texts

This contains a range of units concerned with reading and writing non-fiction texts. By starting with the reading section, you will see how writers use a range of devices to make their writing effective. In the writing section, you will learn how to use these devices and how to structure your writing in a range of different ways. You can further help you work on non-fiction texts by reading newspapers, magazines, autobiographies and travel writing. Each unit takes you through the main points you need to know. There is a practice section at the end. It is a good idea to answer the questions as though you were in an exam. There are lots of reminders to help you work through the book – read them carefully and use the suggestions. You may find it useful to jot notes in the margins on some pages – this is your book! Look at the exam questions and model answers to help you structure your own answers and to give a clear idea of what is expected of you. Study them closely. There is also a glossary at the end of the book, which contains words that may be useful to you in your exam. Make sure you understand all of these.

Planning your revision

Students who get the best grades are those who plan their revision carefully, not those who try to cram it all in at the last minute!

- Make sure you know the date and time of each of your English exams.

- Think about how much time – realistically – you can spend each day and each week on revision. Don't forget that it's not just English you have to revise!

- You may decide to start revision around three months before the exam, in March. This gives you plenty of time to revise a unit at a time. Aim to work in 50-minute sessions with 10-minute intervals.

- Don't just revise something once – go back to it after an hour, then a day, then a week, if you can. This way, you'll become more familiar with the material and more confident.

- Draw up a revision timetable for the days and weeks leading up to the exams, for all your subjects – and stick to it!

- When you sit down to work make sure that:
    - it's quiet
    - you've got everything you need in the room: pens, paper, books and a dictionary
    - you don't get distracted by the telephone or someone else's music
    - you have set yourself a time limit.

Writing for GSCE English

During your GCSE English course, you will be asked to complete a number of writing tasks. These have been grouped into four main areas:

- Writing to explore, imagine, entertain

- Writing to inform, explain, describe

- Writing to argue, persuade, advise

- Writing to analyse, review, comment.

Where you carry out each type of writing depends on the examination syllabus that you are following. Some types are tested in your coursework, others in different papers that you sit at examination time. Whatever type of writing you do, remember to plan and check your writing.

Planning your writing

This is **very** important. You need to:

- gather and jot down a range of ideas that you could include in your writing

- sequence them in the order in which you will write about them

- decide on a paragraph structure

- choose an effective opening and ending for your writing.

Writing for GCSE English *continued*

Checking your work

As you are writing, stop at the end of each paragraph and read back over what you have written. Make sure your writing is still relevant to the question and correct any mistakes.

When you have finished writing, read back over the whole piece. At this stage, you may decide to add some words or cross something out. Check again for any mistakes in spelling or punctuation and correct these.

Whatever examination syllabus you are following, it is essential that you know what is distinct about the type of writing you are going to tackle. BITESIZE English concentrates on writing to argue, persuade and advise. Check with your teacher which other types of writing you need to revise.

On the day

Make sure you know what day the exam is, what time it is and where it is. If you need to take books, such as an anthology, into the exam, make sure you have your copy. There's nothing worse than arriving late and in a fluster only to find you haven't got everything you need.

Get to the exam room in plenty of time. On your way there, go through some of the most important points you need to remember when you start your exam:

■ Read the texts closely.

■ Read the questions carefully.

■ Highlight key words in the questions and key points in the texts.

■ Check how many marks are awarded to each question and use this as a guide for how much you should write.

■ Keep an eye on the time – it's important that you complete all the questions on the paper.

You are now ready to start. We hope you enjoy working with BITESIZE English.

THE BARE BONES

➤ In an examination, include only the material that a question requires.

➤ Always use the <u>PQD</u> method to help you write about texts.

A   Study the writer's work

KEY FACT

Decide which facts and opinions will help you to answer a question.

• As you study the work of a writer, you will come across useful pieces of information that may concern a writer's attitude, background and the cultural influences on his or her life. These are important in your understanding of a writer's work and will assist you in shaping your thoughts.

• However, in the examination you will not be required to write biographical essays. What you are expected to do is to be able to explain how the texts work and why they affect you in the ways that they do.

KEY FACT

Discover the writer's attitude or stance.

• The literature section of this book will give you an understanding of the writer's point of view. You will be given guidance in the shape of some key biographical facts and, more importantly, analysis of the writing itself.

KEY FACT

Discover the language techniques of an author.

• By learning about these techniques, you will be able to demonstrate how effectively a writer expresses thought and feeling. This is important, since the examiners are not testing your knowledge of a subject but your ability to appreciate how a writer achieves certain effects.

B   Analyse the question

KEY FACT

When answering examination questions, the first step is to analyse the question.

• Follow these three key steps:

1 Read the question carefully.

2 Look for the key word or words that tell you what to do.

3 Underline or highlight these words.

C   Prepare your answer carefully

- Here is a sample question:

  'By examining the language of 'Valentine' by Carol Ann Duffy, show how successfully the poet presents her argument.'

- In preparing an answer to this question, there are at least two things to consider:

  1 The main emphasis of the question is on the language, not the content of the poem. You therefore do not need to explain in detail what the poem is about.

  2 In order to decide how successful Duffy is, you must analyse the ways in which she uses language.

- Do not feel you have to make an instant decision. First, find examples of language use. Then make notes on their effect.

D   Set out your answer correctly

- When you come to write your answer, always use the **formula PQD**.

  P stands for the POINT you wish to make.

  Q stands for the QUOTATION to illustrate your point.

  D stands for the DEVELOPMENT of the quotation.

- When answering the above question on Duffy, a good candidate might write:

  In this poem, Duffy treats love in a realistic fashion.
  (Here the candidate is making a good point clearly.)

- Then he or she might write:

  This is shown when she writes:
      'I give you an onion
      Its fierce kiss'.
  (The candidate is supporting the point with a relevant quotation.)

- She or he might then write:

  By referring to the sharp taste of an onion as 'fierce', the poet is not only suggesting how long the 'kiss will stay on your lips', but saying something about the type of kiss. It is not sloppy or romantic, but strong and firm, almost aggressive. It shows that the giver really means it, as in the phrase 'fierce determination'.
  (This is developing the quotation and showing good understanding of meaning.)

- This is the basis of a good essay because, by using the PQD formula, the candidate is able to advance the argument. The examiner will reward a candidate who shows understanding both of the poem and of the right way to tackle an exam question.

Handling quotations
'Cataract operation' by Simon Armitage

THE BARE BONES
➤ When using quotations, set them out correctly.
➤ To do this, use either the PQD formula or brackets in sentences.

A How to find and use quotations

KEY FACT

When writing about poetry, it is important to support the points you make by referring to the text. Follow these stages:

1 Start with a point you wish to make (P).

2 Find a quotation that supports the point you wish to make (Q).

3 Try to develop the point you have just made (D).

KEY FACT

Set out your points and quotations clearly so that the examiner can follow your train of thought. Follow these stages:

1 Write down your point, followed by a colon (:).

2 Start a new paragraph.

3 'Put the quotation in inverted commas.'

4 On the next line, begin your discussion of the quotation.

• Your layout should look like this:

> In 'Cataract operation', the poet is describing how, after an operation to remove a cataract, everything seems very bright: (P)
> 'The sun comes like a head
> through last night's turtleneck'. (Q)
> The use of the simile here suggests that . . .

The examiner is looking to see that you have set out the answer correctly.

KEY FACT

When using a short quotation, place it within your sentence.

• You can use **short quotations**, of less than one line of poetry, to support your argument. Place the words within **quotation marks**. For example:

> When Armitage describes how the pigeon turns and 'offers me a card', he creates a vivid picture of the pigeon's tail feathers as a fan of cards.

B The essential elements

Look for the essential parts of the poet's imagery.
Then think about what they suggest to you.

- Look at the following ideas of what is suggested by key words in the image:

    Sun ⟶ *head, shining brightly, strong light, power*

    Head ⟶ *top, round like sun*

    Turtleneck ⟶ *long neck-like tube, long time for head to push through*

- Now imagine your head inside the sweater. When your head appears through the neck, how would the light strike your eye?

- You could write something like this:

    The use of the simile here reminds you of how, when you put on a turtleneck sweater, at first everything seems <u>dark</u>. But when, <u>eventually</u>, your head appears through the neck, <u>suddenly</u> everything becomes <u>bright</u>, just like when the sun rises.

C Developing the argument

To develop your argument, you need to find a point
that relates directly to the one that you have just made.

- In this example, you could write:

    This is like the sudden restoration of sight that can <u>confuse</u> someone who has just undergone a cataract operation. **(P)**

- The **person being confused** is your new point. It is related to the suddenness with which sight comes back to a patient. A quotation that could be used to support this idea of confusion is:

    'A pigeon in the yard turns tail and offers me a card.' **(Q)**

Q Explain a possible situation where you could be confused by being offered a card.

PRACTICE

1 Show how, in 'Cataract operation', the poet portrays the results of this operation to be rather puzzling. Use the PQD method in your answer.

2 What does Armitage show you about contrasting experiences in 'It ain't what you do'? Use quotations within your sentences when supporting your points.

Comparative study of two poems
'Poem' and 'About his person' by Simon Armitage

THE BARE BONES

➤ When comparing two poems, you need to think about content, i.e. what the poems are about.

➤ You also need to show how meaning is revealed through structure and language.

A Content of a poem

Q What contrasting things does the man in 'Poem' do?

- Both 'Poem' and 'About his person' are concerned with the death of a man: one describes how a man acted during his lifetime; the other is written about a time soon after a man's death. Both poems invite you to draw your own conclusions.

- In 'Poem', Armitage describes some of the things the man did. The reader is left to wonder whether the man was good or bad.

- In 'About his person', the reader is led to believe that the man is dead but is not told how he died.

B Structure of a poem

KEY FACT

The structure of a poem shows you how the poet has organised his or her thoughts and feelings.

Q What do you think about the man in 'Poem'? Give at least three clear reasons for your opinion.

- 'Poem' contains fourteen lines. It is divided into three stanzas of four lines. Each of these sections tells us about things the man did in his life. The last line of each stanza forms a contrast to the first three. Armitage may be trying to influence our judgement by ending each stanza with this contrast.

- The poem ends with a rhyming couplet (two lines that rhyme). They sum up the man's life. The final line uses repetition and is intentionally balanced around the comma, suggesting it is for the reader to decide what kind of man he was.

C The language of symbols

KEY FACT

Symbols may be used by poets to represent what happens to us or how we feel about things.

Remember
Look for symbols in poetry and work out what they represent.

For example: a red rose is often used in poetry as a symbol of love.

- In 'About his person', the poet uses a series of symbols to show us things about the man's life.

- Look at the *'library card'* (line 2), which has a *'date of expiry'*. This tells you when the book is due for return. But the word *'expiry'* can also mean the end or death. So, the expiry date in the library book could represent the death of the man.

D Language and tone

Poets often <u>change the tone</u> to reflect the changing moods in a poem.

- In 'Poem', Armitage is telling a story about a man's life. In lines 3 and 4 he writes:

  *'And always tucked his daughter up at night
  And slippered her the one time she lied.'*

- In the first line, the man comes across as a kind father, but the reader is shocked to learn that he had a harder side to him. This shift of tone changes our response to the man. It keeps the reader alert to different possibilities.

- In 'Poem', Armitage uses a very **matter-of-fact tone**. Lines such as *'And what he didn't spend each week he saved'* (line 6) create an impression of a very ordinary sort of person, living a rather uninteresting life.

- This sense of ordinariness and monotony is reinforced by the use of *'And'* at the start of eleven of the fourteen lines.

PRACTICE

Remember
Focus on words that help to reflect tone and mood.

Copy and complete this chart to highlight the similarities and differences between 'Poem' and 'About his person' with regard to content, structure and use of language.

Title	Content	Structure	Language
Poem	• recounts incidents from man's life • good/bad • relationships with women – daughter/ wife/mother • leaves reader to decide		
About his person			

The poet's viewpoint
'I am very bothered' by Simon Armitage

THE BARE BONES

➤ Sometimes poets speak directly to their readers and their viewpoint is clear.

➤ Sometimes the poet's viewpoint is not immediately clear. The reader has to search the poem for clues.

A Discovering the poet's point of view

KEY FACT

Poets often use a character or 'voice' to show their viewpoint.

1 Persona
They do this by writing in the first person. This is called **adopting a persona**. When you read the untitled poem, *'I am very bothered . . . '*, remember that the 'I' is not necessarily Armitage, the poet. It is the persona that Armitage uses to make the experience sound real.

2 Content
'I am very bothered' describes a trick played in a school chemistry lab. It results in severe burns to a girl's hand and the scars will remain forever. The event is recounted in the first person. It ends with the persona asking the girl not to believe him when he says it was his clumsy way of proposing to her.

3 Thinking about the persona
It is for the reader to decide whether the speaker of this poem intended to harm the girl. There is some evidence for this view, as he seems to revel in the pain he inflicted:

> *'O the unrivalled stench of branded skin'* (line 8).

Alternatively, by writing *'I am very bothered'* and *'Don't believe me please'*, he could be suggesting:

* it was a practical joke gone badly wrong
* he didn't want to marry her then, but he does now.

Remember
You need to look for clues in a poem to help you work out the poet's point of view.

Q What different things does 'butter-fingered' make you think of?

B Structure

* The poem is divided into three stanzas:

  The first stanza is focused on the persona recounting what happened.

  The second stanza shows the effect of the trick on the other person.

  The third stanza returns to the present and how the persona sees the incident now.

* The untitled poem has fourteen lines, and so is a kind of sonnet. Sonnets are often connected with love poetry. You need to decide whether Armitage chose this form because he wanted to write a love poem or because he wanted to mock traditional love poetry.

Q Why do you think Armitage chose the sonnet form for this poem?

c Language

Remember
The tone can change within a poem. To identify the tone, you need to study the words closely.

Q Find evidence to support the idea that the persona is speaking to the person whom he burnt.

- Armitage used to be a probation officer. The first two lines of the poem are written as the reply to a probation officer's question:

  'What kind of things bother you when you look back?'

- The persona replies as though he were speaking to the person he burnt.

- The tone used by the persona changes throughout the poem. The use of the word *'played'* in line 4 suggests this was a game. The tone is light-hearted.

- In line 5, the tone becomes more serious with the words *'naked lilac flame'*. This emphasises how exposed the victim was.

- In the second stanza, the tone of *'O the unrivalled stench'* suggests he took pleasure in what happened.

- In the final stanza, the word *'please'* could suggest that he wants to be taken seriously.

- The image of the *'two burning rings'* reminds the reader of wedding rings, leading to the persona's reference to marriage in the final stanza.

PRACTICE

1 What do you think the persona is trying to say about:
- what happened in the lab
- how he now feels about this incident and the other person?

2 We have assumed the persona is male. Why? Could the persona be female?

3 Think about the poem again. What does the poet, Armitage, seem to be saying about love and relationships? Give reasons for your answer.

The structure of a poem
'It ain't what you do' by Simon Armitage

THE BARE BONES

➤ When examining the structure of a poem, look at how the poet has organised the content.

➤ You will find a poem's structure in the way that language is used.

A Structure through contrasting events

KEY FACT ▸ **The structure indicates how the poem has been built.**

- In the **first stanza**, Armitage compares a person who lives the life of a drop-out with the person who has lived a less glamorous existence. He presents the reader with a series of contrasts.

  For example:

   'I have not bummed across America', 'I have lived with thieves in Manchester'

- In the **second and third stanzas**, he makes a detailed contrast between the Taj Mahal and Black Moss. Copy and complete this chart to highlight the contrasting details:

Place	Action(s)	Tone	Object(s)	Sense(s)
Taj Mahal	padded, listening, picking up, putting down	soft, secretive	marble floor	hearing, touch
Black Moss				

Q Write a few sentences showing the differences between these two people's experiences. Which do you think the writer prefers and why? What other contrasts does Simon Armitage use?

B Structure through similarities

- In the **final stanza**, Armitage suggests that although these experiences seem to be contrasting, they do have similarities. Whether we are doing something exciting or something very ordinary, we still react in a similar way with *'the tightness of the throat'*.

- When you reread the poem carefully, you can find other similarities in the experiences. There is as much sense of danger in living *'with thieves in Manchester'* as there is in *'bumming across America'*.

Q In what ways are the experiences of the Taj Mahal and Black Moss similar?

c   Structure through contrasts in the language

Q How do the
words *'played'*
and *'held'* in the
fourth stanza
emphasise the
contrast
between
parachuting and
the day-centre
activities?

- Armitage uses contrasting words to emphasise the different experiences:

  > The word 'bummed' suggests becoming a drop-out and ignoring social responsibilities.

  > The word 'lived' creates a sense of belonging to and being part of a society, even if it is one of thieves.

- He writes of *'listening'* at the Taj Mahal but of *'hearing'* at Black Moss. *'Listening'* suggests waiting for the experience, whereas hearing gives the experience a sense of reality.

- He uses the word *'but'* to emphasis the contrast:

  > *'I have not padded . . . But I skimmed . . .'*
  > *'I have not toyed . . . but I held . . .'*

- The word *'And'* is used at the start of the final stanza to draw the ideas together.

PRACTICE

1 Armitage ends the poem with: *'That feeling, I mean.'* Which *'feeling'* do you think he is referring to? Explain why you think this.

2 Examine the events and language of 'Poem'. Show how they emphasise the meaning to the poem.

3 Reread 'Poem'. How does Armitage structure his ideas by using:

- contrasts

- similarities?

4 In 'Poem', how does Armitage use the final stanza to sum up his ideas?

Working your way through a poem
'Before you were mine' by Carol Ann Duffy

THE BARE BONES

➤ You can understand a poem through its structure.

➤ You can understand a poem by examining its language.

➤ The four stanzas of 'Before you were mine' deal with the relationship of the poet and her mother at different times in their lives.

A   The structure of time in the four stanzas

KEY FACT

> **Q** Why did Duffy give her mother the nickname 'Marilyn'?

1   The <u>first</u> stanza concerns a time before Duffy was born.

- Duffy writes about a time before she was born (*'ten years away'*). She imagines her mother playing with some of her friends. She uses the present tense, as though everything is happening now.
- The memories are action-packed and noisy (*'bend'*, *'blows round'*, *'shriek'*). This makes them vivid. She wants to possess: *'I wanted the bold girl.'*

KEY FACT

> **Q** Which phrase shows how Duffy instinctively understands her mother?

2   The <u>second</u> stanza shows her mother at a later stage in her life.

- Duffy is still not born (*'I'm not here yet'*). Her mother is pictured in her teenage years. Her visits to the pictures give her romantic visions of finding Mr Right (*'movie tomorrows/the right walk home could bring'*). Notice how *'movie'* links with *'Marilyn'* in the first stanza.
- The lights from the glitter ball over the dance floor could represent the eyes of men watching her. Duffy introduces her mother's own mother (*'your Ma stands at the close'*). This introduces another time-scale into the poem.

KEY FACT

> **Q** What does Duffy mean by *'ghost'* in line 15?

3   The <u>third</u> stanza concentrates on the poet's memories.

- Duffy is now ten years old (*'decade ahead'*). Notice how at birth Duffy wanted to control her mother. Her first cry is a *'possessive yell'*.
- The poet's memories are made very real by describing them through the senses (*'my hands in'*, *'clear as scent'*, *'small bites'*).

KEY FACT

> **Q** Reread the poem. What have you learnt about Duffy's relationship with her mother?

4   The <u>fourth</u> stanza focuses on the memories of times spent together.

- These are lively and loving memories of the mother teaching her daughter dance steps when they were coming home from church. The memories remain in the *'sparkle'*, the *'waltz'* and the *'laugh'*. But Duffy wants more than memories. She wants to possess: *'I wanted the bold girl.'*

B Structure through language

Remember
Duffy can write imaginatively about experience in very practical and down-to-earth terms.

Q Select some phrases. Say if they are imaginative, realistic or both.

1 The poem is based on a **paradox** (see Glossary). The puzzle is seen first in the title of the poem. We normally think about a daughter belonging to her mother. But Duffy switches the roles. She wants to possess her mother.

2 For everyday memories, the language is **colloquial**: *'you laugh on/with your pals.'* (lines 1–2). The **tone** is that of **everyday conversation**: *'You reckon it's worth it'* (line 11).

3 Through Duffy's **imagination**, the language becomes more **poetic**: *'in the ballroom with the thousand eyes'* (line 7).

4 Sometimes, Duffy combines the **poetic** and the **matter-of-fact**: *'now your ghost clatters'* (line 15). Normally, you would expect a ghost to be ethereal, other-worldly, but this ghost belongs to this world all right!

PRACTICE

1 What do each of these phrases tell you about what attracted Duffy to her mother?

> *your polka-dot dress blows round your legs*
> *in the ballroom with the thousand eyes*
> *small bites on your neck*
> *the bold girl winking in Portobello*
> *where you sparkle and waltz and laugh*

2 The title of the poem is 'Before you were mine'. In the fourth stanza, Duffy *'wanted the bold girl'*. From what you have read in the poem, why do you think Duffy wanted her mother so much?

Understanding issues
'War photographer' by Carol Ann Duffy

THE BARE BONES

➤ Duffy raises important issues about the media, and people's response to it, in 'War photographer'.

➤ The war photographer inhabits two very different, contrasting worlds.

A Important media issues raised in the poem

1 Political and religious issues
In the first stanza, Duffy lists three political trouble spots. **Belfast** in Northern Ireland is an area of conflict between peoples of different religions. **Phnom Penh** in Cambodia is an example of western powers becoming politically involved in another country's war. The fighting in **Beirut** in the Lebanon was caused by the fierce rivalry of political and religious groups.

2 The issue of responsibility
The war photographer makes a living by taking pictures of human suffering. But he has a sense of responsibility towards the paper's readers. He does this difficult job so that they can see the truth of what is happening. Duffy gives the job a religious significance.

3 The issue of suffering
The poem presents **two types of suffering**. There is the physical suffering of people caught up in war: *'the blood stained into foreign dust'* (line 18). There is also the suffering the photographer feels when he looks at his photographs: *'He remembers the cries'* (line15). This is contrasted with the short-lived tears of the readers in the final stanza.

4 Personal issues
The photographer inhabits **two different worlds**. The world at home, *'Rural England'*, is peaceful with *'ordinary pain'*. But abroad he is engaged on dangerous assignments and the pain is not ordinary. The photographs he takes are described as *'A hundred agonies in black and white'.*

5 Professional issues
Each profession has its own **code of conduct**. The photographer has a duty to the people he photographs and to the paper's readers. In line 16 *'he sought approval'* of a man's wife before taking a photograph of her husband's suffering. The editor must decide which photographs to print. Some pictures may cause the readers distress (*'The reader's eyeballs prick'*, line 21). But will the effect last after *'the pre-lunch beers'* (line 22)?

6 The issues of reality
In the **last two lines** of the poem, it is not clear whether the photographer is staring *'impassively'* (without emotion) at England or at the country at war. He earns his living in both countries and there is evidence in the poem that in both places *'they do not care'*.

Q How do we know that the photographer finds his job difficult?

Q What other things do you learn about the two worlds and the differences between them?

Q How did the photographer seek the wife's approval? How do you think he felt at that time?

Q What do you think Duffy means by *'care'*? What evidence is there that the people in both countries do not care?

B Language of the poem

Duffy presents these media issues through the language of the poem.

1 Choice of words represent two different worlds

The world of home is felt to be calm and uncomplicated. The language reflects this: the rows are *'ordered'* (line 2); the pain is *'ordinary'*, the weather *'simple'* (line 10). On the other hand, the words chosen to express the overseas assignments are violent: *'explode'* (line 11) and *'nightmare heat'* (line 12).

2 Use of ambiguous language

She does this to show the predicament of the war photographer. In line 7, the word *'solutions'* has two meanings.

One meaning is the liquid used by the photographer to develop a negative. The solution makes the photographic image clear.

Another meaning concerns the solving of problems. In other words, how can the problem of suffering be solved?

By using the ambiguous word *'solutions'*, Duffy suggests that the prints developed in the darkroom may have something important to say about suffering.

3 Use of religious comparisons

In the first stanza, Duffy suggests that the war photographer's job takes on a sense of religious importance. She compares him developing the spools of film to a priest getting ready for a service. The red light of the developing room ensures that the film is not ruined, and it *'softly glows as though this were a church'*.

PRACTICE

1 'War photographer' raises many issues. What are the issues for the newspaper readers? What are the issues for the subjects of the photographs? Give reasons for your answers.

2 What do the following phrases tell you about the photographer's different worlds?

His world back home	His world of foreign assignments
half-formed ghost	explode beneath their feet
ordinary pain	nightmare heat
simple weather	the cries of this man's wife
half-formed ghost	blood stained into foreign dust

Reading between the lines
'Stealing' by Carol Ann Duffy

THE BARE BONES

➤ The surface meaning of a poem can be discovered on the first or second reading.

➤ To find the deeper meaning, you need to read between the lines by looking at language and context.

A Looking for surface meaning

KEY FACT

Look for meaning in the way a poem is told.

Remember
Search for meaning in what the thief tells us.

1 'Stealing' is based on an actual incident.

• Duffy was living on Wimbledon Common in London at the time when a snowman was stolen.

• In the poem, she gives the imagined thief a voice. Duffy allows the thief to tell the story in a colloquial, off-hand manner: *'The most unusual thing I ever stole'*.

• The reader learns about the thief's character by the way the story is told.

Q Find two other examples of the way the poem is told. What do they suggest about the thief's character?

2 Read what the thief says.

• The thief describes events in a **straightforward manner**: *'I started with the head . . . He weighed a ton . . . I took a run and booted him.'*

• Many of the thief's reasons for stealing are quite explicit: *'He looked magnificent.'*

• But when you read *'I wanted him'*, you begin to ask questions about the identity of the thief. We are not told whether the thief is a teenager or an adult, a man or woman. It is left for the reader to decide on the evidence given in the poem.

B Looking for deeper meaning

KEY FACT

Read between the lines to find the deeper meaning.

1 Think about what the thief says and does.

• The thief says he wanted *'a mate with a mind as cold as the slice of ice within my own brain'*. This could suggest that the thief is lonely and feels frozen inside, as though without warmth and feeling.

Q Why do you think the thief stole the snowman?

• Some of the thief's attitudes to life, such as *'Better off dead than giving in'*, are puzzling and raise questions. Better than what? Giving in to what? Other comments such as *'life's tough'* suggest things about the thief's own background and upbringing.

Q What other things do you learn about the thief from what he says and does?

• The thefts referred to in lines 11–13 introduce another idea. Things are done *'just to have a look'*. Here the thief is shown to be a **voyeur**.

• Duffy reinforces this idea of the thief as an observer rather than a doer with the words *'I watched my gloved hand . . .'* later in the same stanza.

B

2 Think about the context.

- In line 15, the word *'Mirrors'* stands isolated. The surface meaning here is not clear.

- To help solve the problem, look for meaning in the context of the surrounding words. They are:

    > *'I watch my gloved hand twisting the doorknob.*
    > *A stranger's bedroom. Mirrors. I sigh like this – Aah.'*

- Ask yourself questions about the details:

    Why does the thief watch his/her hand?

    Why is the hand *'gloved'*?

    What does the word *'twisting'* add to the theft?

    What is suggested by writing *'bedroom'* door as opposed to, say, dining-room door?

    In this situation why might the thief sigh?

    What kind of a sigh do you think it is?

- Also, ask yourself why the thief might be interested in mirrors. To help you, think about why different people use mirrors.

    Your answers to these questions might suggest: an actor, a voyeur, a lover, a person obsessed with his or her own self.

3 Examine different sides of the thief's character.

- A **sadistic** side: *'Part of the thrill was knowing/that children would cry in the morning.'* (lines 9–10)

- A **callous**, unthinking side: *'I took a run and booted him again.'* (lines 17–18)

- A **better** side, someone with a conscience: *'It seems daft now.'* (line 19)

- A **ridiculous**, pitiable side: *'standing alone amongst lumps of snow'.* (line 20)

- A **disillusioned** side: *'sick of the world'.* (line 20)

Remember
Use the context to find the deeper meaning.

PRACTICE

1 What do the following tell you about the different sides of the thief's nature?

> *'I stole a guitar and thought I might/learn to play'*
> *'I nicked a bust of Shakespeare once/flogged it'*

2 The thief ends by saying: *'You don't understand a word I'm saying, do you?'*
How does reading between the lines help you to understand what the thief, and the poet, are trying to say?

Looking at language

'In Mrs Tilscher's class' and 'Valentine' by Carol Ann Duffy

THE BARE BONES

➤ Duffy uses language in different ways to get her meaning across.

➤ You can develop your understanding of a poem by giving more attention to the tone of the language.

A How Duffy uses language in different ways

KEY FACT

Remember
Duffy uses language to create a vivid picture of the classroom.

1 Language is used to structure a poem.

- 'In Mrs Tilscher's class' is written in the first person (I, we) as though it were an autobiographical account of a final year of primary school.

- Duffy uses a framework of words associated with school, such as *'tracing'*, *'chanted'* and *'chalky'*. This creates a vivid picture of Mrs Tilscher's classroom.

KEY FACT

Q What is suggested by *'a good gold star'*, *'the scent of a pencil'* and *'a xylophone's nonsense'*?

2 Language is used to create mood.

- In the **first stanza**, the mood is playful and joyful, with words such as *'skittle of milk'* and *'laugh of a bell'*.

- There is a slight change in the **second stanza**. Although the classroom still glowed *'like a sweetshop'*, there is a hint of danger in the outside adult world, with the reference to Brady and Hindley, the Moors Murderers. The image of an *'uneasy smudge of a mistake'* suggests that they can never be completely forgotten.

- She comes face to face with the facts of life: *'inky tadpoles changed from commas into exclamation marks'.*

KEY FACT

Q What do *'feverish'* and *'fractious'* tell you about the atmosphere at school?

3 Language is used to show change.

- The idea of change is introduced at the start of the **third stanza** as *'the inky tadpoles changed/from commas into exclamation marks'*. This suggests growing up.

- The visual image also reflects the increased competence of the children in the use of punctuation. There is perhaps a hint of warning in the use of the exclamation mark.

- In the **final stanza**, Duffy uses language to create a sense of danger and tension. The *'air tasted of electricity'* and there is a *'tangible alarm'*. The developing child is reaching sexual awareness. The sheltered world of the classroom is being left behind. This sense of danger is reinforced in the final line of the poem: *'as the sky split open into a thunderstorm'*.

B How Duffy explores love and relationships in 'Valentine'

EY FACT ▶

1 Duffy uses the image of an onion as a valentine's gift to explore a changing relationship.

- Duffy was sitting in her kitchen, worrying about finding a suitable subject for a poem that she had been commissioned to write for Valentine's Day. Then she spotted an onion. She started to think about words and ideas associated with this.

- In the poem, the speaker describes the onion as a *'moon wrapped in brown paper'* and the peeling of it as the *'careful undressing of love'*.

- The **second stanza** opens with the onion making her lover cry and becoming *'a wobbling photo of grief'*. The idea of it *'blinding you with tears'* reminds the reader of the idea that love is blind. In sending a real, if unusual valentine, she is trying to be truthful.

Q What do you associate with these words: *blind, wobbling, cute*?

EY FACT ▶

Remember Duffy uses tone to show the different aspects of a relationship.

2 Duffy changes the tone to match the changing relationship.

- The poem opens with a light, humorous tone. Lines 13–17 introduce a sense of passion but also danger with the words *'fierce'* and *'possessive'*.

- In the final stanza, the word *'shrink'* is used to describe how the onion becomes smaller. This suggests that the love is also diminished and less important to the speaker.

- The sense of danger is also reinforced in this stanza with the word *'lethal'*. This introduces an atmosphere of foreboding and murderous thoughts. The knife, which has been used to peel away the onion layers, could be an instrument of death.

Q What is suggested by the use of '*cling*' in the final stanza? Why do you think Duffy repeats this word?

PRACTICE

1 How does Duffy use language to create a vivid picture of a place in 'In Mrs Tilscher's class'? Remember to refer closely to the poem to support the points you make.

2 Write about the way Duffy uses the image of an onion to explore a relationship in 'Valentine'. You should write about:

- the ways in which the relationship is compared to an onion
- the ways in which the relationship changes
- the effectiveness of this image.

Finding the meaning

'Hawk roosting' by Ted Hughes

THE BARE BONES

➤ To find the meaning of this poem, you need to understand the persona of the hawk.

➤ You should be aware of the relationship between nature and the nature of the bird.

A Examining the persona of the hawk

KEY FACT

Poets often speak through another person. This is called adopting a <u>persona</u>.

1 Here a hawk is used as the persona. The hawk is the speaker and everything is seen from his perspective. The opening word '*I*' emphasises his central role.

2 The reader learns about the bird through his appearance and his behaviour. In the first stanza, we learn that the bird has a '*hooked head*' and '*hooked feet*'. The repetition of the word '*hooked*' emphasises his power. This is reinforced by the fact that he uses his hooked feet to '*tear off heads*'.

3 The hawk's stance emphasises his importance. He is sitting '*in the top of the wood*', a situation that reflects his superiority. It is as though he were looking down on every other living creature.

His arrogance is shown when he says:

> '*It took the whole of Creation*
> *To create my foot, my each feather*.'

This suggests how important the bird is. If it took the whole of creation to make parts of his body, how long must it have taken to create all of him?

Remember
You need to explore the persona of the hawk.

Q Find examples of statements where the poet uses the words '*I*' and '*my*' to emphasise the fact that it is the bird who is speaking.

Q What other things do you learn about the hawk's appearance and behaviour?

B   The hawk and nature

The relationship between the hawk and nature is revealing.

1 The world of nature and the world of the hawk are both present in the poem. As you study the poem, decide whether:

- nature controls the hawk
- the hawk controls nature
- both statements are true.

2 The hawk's environment reveals more things about the hawk. It is suggested that it is there for the benefit of the hawk:

'The air's buoyancy' suggests the elements help the bird to stay in the sky.

'The convenience of the high trees' shows how the environment benefits the bird, in giving it a vantage point.

'The sun is behind me' implies that the sun gives him an advantage when attacking prey and that he is greater than the sun.

3 The tone of the language tells you important things about the relationship between the world of nature and the world of the hawk. Consider what the bird says about himself: *'I kill where I please'* and *'My manners are tearing off heads'.* Does the tone of these statements suggest he is:

- a creature acting on instinct
- behaving like a human being who has been brought up to act in a certain way
- acting the role of a king looking down on his kingdom? (The Elizabethans thought nature was a society that worked because every creature had its particular place. In the bird kingdom, the hawk was king.)

Q Find another example in the second stanza of the hawk's belief that nature is there for his convenience.

PRACTICE

Complete the following chart to identify how the hawk:

- thinks   • regards himself.

Quotation	What the hawk is saying	What it suggests about the way the hawk sees himself
I kill where I please because it is all mine *There is no sophistry in my body* *No arguments assert my rights* *Nothing has changed since I began* *I am going to keep things like this.*		

The poet and nature
'The warm and the cold' by Ted Hughes

THE BARE BONES

➤ To understand the poet's attitude towards nature, you should be aware of the structure of a poem.

➤ Hughes makes extensive use of similes to describe how the different creatures survive the frost.

A The structure of the poem

KEY FACT

Q Which different creatures does Hughes refer to in this poem?

The overall structure is built around nature's different forms.

It is built around:

• the world in which we live

• creatures of land, sea and air

• the nature of a creature

• human nature.

KEY FACT

Q What do you think Hughes is saying about nature's different forms?

The stanzas follow a strict pattern.
The first three stanzas contain:

• four lines that set the scene followed by a contrasting: *'But . . .'*

• eight lines of similes containing examples of creatures surviving the cold.

The contrast is sustained at the end of the poem, with the night *'frost'* and the *'sweating farmers'.*

B How the language structure supports the meaning

KEY FACT

Similes, rhyme and rhythm form the basis of the structure.

• The similes are thumbnail sketches of creatures in the worlds of water and earth.

For example:

'the badger in its bedding' (line 7)
'the cod is in the tide rip' (line 29)

• The rhymes build up a regular rhythm.

For example:

'Like a viol in its case . . .
'Like a doll in its lace.' (lines 10 and 12)
'Like a key in a purse . . .
'Like smiles on a nurse.' (lines 30 and 32)

Q What do the images of the *'freezing dusk'* suggest about a winter's night?

B

- The similes used to describe the freezing dusk are violent in tone.

For example:

'*Like a slow trap of steel*' (line 2)
'*Like a nut screwed tight*' (line 14)

Hughes presents the reader with a series of puzzles to solve.

Think about what he means by:

'*And the badger in its bedding
Like a loaf in the oven*' (lines 7–8)

To explain this puzzle, identify the key words: '*bedding*', '*loaf*' and '*oven*'.

Find similarities between them. One similarity is heat, the bedding being warm and the loaf being very hot.

So, your explanation of the simile might be:

The poet compares the badger's situation to that of a loaf in an oven. In this way he emphasises the warmth and cosiness of the animal's bedding.

EY FACT

Q Using the same method, explain these:

- *Sparrows are in the ivy-clump*
- *Like a key in the purse*
- *Like money in a pig.*

PRACTICE

Identifying the tone can help you to understand the meaning.

Read the following words that could be used to describe the tone at different stages of the poem:

disturbed   humorous   threatening   puzzling   comforting
homely   positive   negative   menacing   sinister   jolly

Now complete the following chart by identifying what each simile suggests and its tone. The first one has been done for you.

Comparison	What is being described	What the comparison suggests	Tone of the comparison
'Like a slow trap of steel'	freezing dusk closing	suffering and torture	threatening, sinister
'Like a planet in its heaven'			
'Like a nut screwed tight'			
'Like a chuckle in a sleeper'			
'Like a clock in its tower'			
'Like smiles on a nurse'			
'Like oxen on spits'			

Looking at language
'Tractor' by Ted Hughes

THE BARE BONES

➤ Hughes uses a range of language features to get his ideas across.
➤ When writing about Hughes's poetry, you need to be able to comment on how he uses language.

Read the poem out loud to appreciate how Hughes uses language.

This will help you feel the frustrations of trying to start the tractor on a freezing morning. You will become more aware of how the poet created this feeling.

KEY FACT

1   Onomatopoeia is used to create the sounds the tractor makes.

- Hughes uses **onomatopoeia** (see Glossary) to represent mechanical noises. Listen to the sounds: *'coughs'*, *'jabbers'*, *'screeched'*, *'raging'*, *'trembling'*.

KEY FACT

2   At times, Hughes combines metaphor with onomatopoeia.

- A **metaphor** is a comparison between two objects or ideas contained in one word. For example, *'the ship ploughed through the waves'*. The word *'ploughed'* likens the ship cutting through water to a plough cutting through earth. It shows the reader how to view the ship.

- Hughes uses a metaphor for the tractor when he writes *'it just coughs'*. A cough is a short sound made by a human. In this poem, it represents the short sound an engine makes when it tries to fire. Just as a cough is an irritation to someone who has a cold, so the engine's failure to start is an irritation to the poet.

Remember
When writing about metaphors and similes, you must explain the effect they have and how this is created.

KEY FACT

3   Hughes uses a combination of metaphors and similes.

- In a **simile**, one thing is compared with another. The words **like** or **as** are usually used to make the comparison. For example, *'hands are like wounds'*. By comparing hands to wounds, Hughes helps the reader to understand the extent of the pain.

Q List other metaphors and similes.

KEY FACT

4   Hughes uses paradox.

- A **paradox** is a statement that appears to contradict itself. Hughes uses the paradox *'white heat of numbness'* to show how in winter, hands that have been frozen suddenly feel as though they are burning.

Q Explain these paradoxes: *'smoking snow'* (line 4), *'laughing pain'* (line 33).

EY FACT

Q Explain
these examples
of
personification:
'It ridicules me'
(line 29),
*'the tractor
streaming with
sweat'* (line 54).

5 Through personification, Hughes gives life to an object.

- This helps the reader to see the tractor as a living creature that is deliberately in conflict with Hughes.

For example:

> *'I squirt commercial sure-fire*
> *Down the black throat – it just coughs.'*

- You could explain the way the personification works thus:

> The use of 'throat' makes the act of squirting sound painful. It sounds as though Hughes is attacking a human being. He seems to be losing his temper and wants to get his own back on the tractor. The tractor's reaction, 'it just coughs', shows how little effect Hughes has on it.

EY FACT

6 Hughes uses <u>alliteration</u> and <u>assonance</u> to increase the power of his writing.

The examiner is looking for answers that explain the alliteration and assonance.

Alliteration is the repetition of the same or similar consonants.

Example: *'As if the <u>t</u>oe-nails were all just <u>t</u>orn off'*

Explanation: the repetition of the 't' sound echoes the 't' in torture and makes the suffering sound more agonising.

Assonance is the repetition of the same or similar vowel sounds.

Example: *'<u>A</u>s if it were h<u>a</u>mmering <u>a</u>nd h<u>a</u>mmering'*

Explanation: The repetition of the 'a' sound in *'As hammering and hammering'* serves to emphasise the repeated hammer blows.

PRACTICE

Look at this chart. Complete the second column to show how the comparison works and the third column to explain the effect of the comparison:

Metaphor/simile	Comparison	Effect
hands are like wounds	wounds suggests deep, painful cuts and sores	helps reader to understand extent of pain
its open entrails		
As if the toe-nails were all just torn off		
hell of ice		
streaming with sweat		

Sound and rhythm
'Wind' and 'Work and play' by Ted Hughes

THE BARE BONES

➤ Hughes uses alliteration, assonance and rhythm in his poetry to create certain effects.

➤ Hughes varies line length to match his subject matter.

A   **'Wind'** by Ted Hughes

KEY FACT

> Hughes uses key devices to create a sense of the power of the wind.

Remember
Read the poems aloud to appreciate the power.

Try reading the poem aloud to help you appreciate his technique.

1 Ted Hughes generates a sense of the wind's power by combining the sounds of words and their rhythm. The power of the wind is established in the first stanza: *'The woods crashing through darkness, the booming hills.'*

By letting the rhythmic beat fall on *'crashing'* and *'booming'*, Hughes emphasises the noise that words make. This, in turn, gives emphasis to the sound of the wind. This combination of rhythm and sound gives the poem its driving force.

Q Explain what meaning the use of alliteration and assonance give to the following:

'Blade-light, luminous black and emerald Back gull bent like an iron bar slowly Rang like some fine green goblet.'

2 Alliteration and assonance are used to emphasise the sense of the wind's power. Listen to the various sounds in: *'Floundering <u>bla</u>ck <u>a</u>stride <u>and</u> <u>bl</u>inding wet'.*

The hammer blows of the repeated letter 'b' give the line its energy. The repetition of the 'a' sound in *'black astride and'* keeps the line steady until the next blow (*'blinding'*) is *'felt'*. The line recreates the feeling of being caught in a gale.

3 Rhythm in English verse works on a stress system. Some syllables are stressed (emphasised) while others are unstressed.

The stress is denoted by a forward slash (/). By putting the mark on a stressed syllable, you can denote the rhythm. In Hughes's verse, much of the power comes from the rhythm.

    /   /   /   /   /   /
Through the brunt wind that dented the balls of my eyes

The rhythm is like a series of hammer blows, emphasising the repeated gusts of wind.

B 'Work and play' by Ted Hughes

Hughes uses a combination of rhythm, alliteration and varied line length to maintain a balance between work and play.

1 The rhythm is regular, hypnotic, like the flight of a bird. Each line is divided into equal halves by a comma. This emphasises the even movement of the bird.

> /   /   /   /
> *The swallow of summer, she toils all the summer*
> /   /   /   /
> *The swallows of summer, the seamstress of summer*

2 Short lines are used to emphasise the discomfort of the holiday people. Consider the following:

> /   /
> *And <u>start</u> up the <u>serpent</u>*
> /   /
> *And <u>head</u>ache it <u>home</u>ward*

The lines are shorter, but sound and rhythm are still used to structure the verse. The **stress** falls on the **alliteration** to emphasise the holiday people's discomfort.

3 Hughes varies the **line length** according to need. A long line emphasises the amount of time it takes to drive onto the beach and find a parking spot:

> *'But the serpent of cars that collapsed on the beach'.*

This is followed by a very short line: *'Disgorges its organs'*, which emphasises how quickly they get out of the car.

PRACTICE

1 Write about the different techniques that Hughes uses to convey the power of the wind in 'Wind'.

2 Write about how Hughes uses rhythm and line length to emphasise the differences between the swallow and the holiday people.

Cultures within a culture
from 'Unrelated incidents' by Tom Leonard

THE BARE BONES

➤ The way we speak is an important part of our cultural identity.

➤ Standard English and Received Pronunciation are features of the way newsreaders traditionally speak.

➤ There can be humour in the use of an accent.

A Standard English and Received Pronunciation

1 Before **standard English**, everybody spoke the **dialect** of their own area. Because the government and major universities were situated in the south-east of England, this area was felt to be very important. The accent of these educated, powerful people came to be the dominant one in England.

People who wanted to get on in life adapted their speech to fit in. This accent came to be known as **Received Pronunciation**

This language development had a cultural effect. Those who used Received Pronunciation were considered superior to the rest of the community. Their opinions were thought to carry more weight than those of people who spoke with an accent. Most newscasters on national television and radio used Received Pronunciation.

2 Received Pronunciation is neutral in tone. It suggests the speaker is educated. To some, a dialect may sound uneducated and common. A prejudiced listener may conclude that the first carries authority and the second doesn't.

3 The words in the poem are written phonetically to show the way they are pronounced by the newsreader.

> **For example:**
> 'iz coz yi
> widny wahnt
> mi ti talk.'
>
> If this were written in standard English, it would be:
> 'is because you
> wouldn't want
> me to talk.'

4 The speaker is making an attack on those who believe that if you do not speak with Received Pronunciation, you have nothing worth saying. He assumes the role of the newsreader but speaks with a strong Glaswegian accent. He makes it clear that he has something important to say:

> 'this/is ma trooth.'

5 The punctuation in the poem is almost random, with no use of capital letters. The poet perhaps chose to present the words in this way to reinforce the idea of spoken English or to suggest a lack of education.

Q 'Unrelated incidents' supposes a newsreader with a strong regional accent. Try reading the poem aloud. You might find it amusing, but has it a serious side?

Q Choose any four lines of the poem. Rewrite them in standard English.

B The effects of speaking with an accent

Writers can use accents to create humour.

Some of the reasons for accents sounding comical are:

- The listener thinks he knows how a person should sound in a certain situation.
- We all tend to think that other people should speak as we do.
- A person might use Received Pronunciation to sound posh.
- We tend to give excuses for the way we speak.
- We do not really know how we sound to others.

Look at the following examples from the poem. We can see which of these reasons could be used to explain the comic effect:

thi reason a talk wia BBC accent (lines 5–8)	He may think he is using Received Pronunciation but, clearly, he is not. He is actually trying to give an excuse for the way he speaks! He certainly does not know how he sounds to others.
wia voice lik wanna you scruff. (lines 12–15)	We know how a newsreader should sound and this reader is not fulfilling our expectations. He does not know how he sounds to others.

The audience is affected by the way a broadcaster speaks.

Think about the poem. What kind of audience is the speaker addressing? He probably thinks he is talking to people from a different background to his own. He may consider himself superior to his audience.

You may think it is important for a speaker to use the same accent as his audience. It is for this reason that many local TV and radio stations employ newscasters with regional accents.

PRACTICE

1 Separate out the different points the speaker makes and list them in standard English.

2 What is the speaker saying about attitudes to accent and dialect?

3 What point do you think the poet is trying to make?

4 Do you think newsreaders should speak in regional accents or with Received Pronunciation? Give your reasons.

THE BARE BONES

➤ We can learn about a culture through what is said and how it is said.

➤ Language is an important part of our cultural identity, as shown in 'Search for my tongue'.

A 'Half-caste' by John Agard

KEY FACT

There are many influences on the language used in a culture.

1 In 'Half-caste', the persona uses two different languages: West Indian Patois **and** standard English.

> **For example:**
>
> *mix in de sky* (Patois)
> *is a half-caste weather* (Standard English)
> *wid a white key* (Patois)
> *is a half-caste symphony* (Standard English).

This emphasises that the persona's origins rest in two halves.

2 Primarily, culture defines a person's origins.

• Your culture comes from where you were brought up and how you were influenced.

• Culture can also be something that is added, something that you consciously decide to accept. So, culture can be seen as artistic expression, in painting and in music.

• The West Indian persona gives two examples from European culture: **Picasso** and **Tchaikovsky**. Because they began in a different culture but have come into his own, he calls them 'half-caste'. Picasso is half-caste because he mixes two colours, red and green. Tchaikovsky is half-caste, in that he mixes *'a black key/wid a white key'* (lines 28–9).

• Through these images, the persona is mocking the whole idea that anyone can be half-caste. He is also showing by these references that he is a 'cultured' person.

3 Agard emphasises the idea of cultural separation by his use of the word 'half'.

• One half of him listens: *'Ah listening to yuh wid de keen/half of mih ear'* (lines 33–4). He sees with half his eye: *'de keen/half of mih eye'* (lines 35–6). He offers *'half-a-hand'* (line 39) and sleeps with *'half-a-eye'* (line 41).

• He continues to build on this image until lines 48–50, when the reader is told to come back with the whole of his eye, ear and mind. The poet is suggesting that people who use the term half-caste in a racist way are not using their eyes, ears and mind properly.

Q Find and write down other examples of the persona mixing standard English and dialect.

Remember
A person's culture can be influenced by people from different cultures.

Q What do you think the poet means by:
'I will tell yu/de other half/of my story'?

Q Find other examples of the poet using the word 'half' to emphasise the point he is making.

A 4 The tone affects the language.

- The poem starts with a mock apology: *'Excuse me.'*

- He feels incomplete (*'standing on one leg'*). But the tone changes as he quickly moves onto the attack (*'Explain yuself'*).

- He uses this phrase to punctuate the logical argument.

Q What do you notice about tone used in the Picasso and Tchaikovsky comparisons?

B *from* 'Search for my tongue' *by Sujata Bhatt*

KEY FACT

Cultures come from language.

1 In 'Search for my tongue', the sense of cultural difference is expressed through language.

- The poet presents her argument in standard English: *'I ask you, what would you do?'* (line 3), but she is suffering a cultural predicament. She has lost her mother tongue. Only in a dream is she aware of her first language, her mother tongue, Gujerati.

- When Bhatt uses this language in the middle section of the poem, she spells the sounds phonetically in English. The reader is made to experience what it feels like to be faced with a foreign 'tongue'.

2 Bhatt uses the tongue as a symbol of cultural identity.

- She wonders what you would do with two tongues in your mouth, these representing her native language and the language of the country to which she has moved.

- She also likens her native language to a plant that would *'rot and die in you mouth.'*

- In lines 31–4, after the dream, Bhatt suggests the tongue has grown back as *'a stump of a shoot'.* She traces the different stages of the tongue's new growth through the symbols of **stump**, **bud** and **shoot**.

- The conflict of the tongues is finally resolved as her mother tongue *'blossoms'* out of her mouth. This image of flowering shows her delight in the return of her mother tongue.

Remember Bjhatt uses the two tongues to represent her native language and the new language that she now uses.

Q Explain the argument the poet makes in lines 1–16 of the poem.

PRACTICE

1 What does Agard seem to be saying about people who call others 'half-caste'? Give five separate points in your answer. Support each point by referring to the text.

2 Explain how Bhatt uses the symbol of tongues to explore how it feels to move to a foreign country where you have to speak a different language.

THE BARE BONES

➤ In 'Presents from my aunts in Pakistan', clothes are used as a symbol of the culture that the poet has left behind.

➤ You can tell how the poet views her past and present cultures by the way she responds to the clothes that she has been sent.

KEY FACT

Remember
The poet expresses her cultural loyalties through clothing.

Q What colours are used in the first stanza? What image do they give?

Q How does the poet feel about her parents camel-skin lamp?

Q How do each of the following phrases imply a feeling of separation: *'wrapping them in tissue'*, *'staring through fretwork'*?

Culture is presented in different ways in the poem.

1 Culture is shown to be a divisive influence.

• The poem shows the writer as being caught between two cultures. She lives in the West but looks back to her origins in Pakistan.

• The phrase *'of no fixed nationality'* (line 66) expresses her predicament. She neither belongs to her original culture, nor to the one she finds around her in England.

2 Culture is revealed through visual symbols.

• The clash of cultures is shown chiefly by comparing women's dress and jewellery in different societies.

• The first stanza describes the vivid colours of female dress in Pakistan. Her loose-fitting trousers, the salwar kameez, are seen as attractive. They glisten like *'an orange split open'*.

• But there is a darker side. The bangles she is given *'snapped, drew blood'*. So, although she finds her original culture attractive, there are disadvantages.

3 A culture can be felt to be alien.

• The poet says how she feels *'alien'* wearing the clothes she has been sent. It is as though they do not belong in her adopted country.

• She expresses her preference for *'denim'* and *'corduroy'*. These represent her cultural position now. Her preference for western fashion makes her original culture seem alien and foreign.

• The clothes were *'radiant in my wardrobe'* (line 37). This suggests that although she finds her original culture attractive, she keeps it hidden away.

4 History helps to define culture.

• Her clothes and the glasswork remind her of the time when she first sailed to England.

• The words *'sailed'* and *'fifties' photographs'* indicate how long ago this was.

• The phrase *'prickly heat'* suggests that the journey, the change from one culture to another, was uncomfortable. She was leaving a society of traditional customs. In Lahore women lived separately, *'screened from male visitors'*.

5 The poem's structure emphasises the cultural gap.

- The poem opens with a statement of fact: *'They sent me'*.
- The next stanza begins with a statement of fact: *'I tried each'*.
- The tone shifts in the next three stanzas: *'I longed'*, *'I wanted'*, *'My mother cherished'*. Thus the poem moves from the situation as it is or was, to the poet expressing what she really wants. The tone expresses her keen desire for change.

6 Her reaction to fashion and clothing symbolises her cultural position.

- Throughout the poem, the poet expresses feelings of cultural uncertainty.
- This is often expressed in the way her clothes fit. Difficulties are hinted at early in the poem: *'snapped,' 'broad and stiff'*. The clothes are a *'costume'*.
- Nevertheless, her eastern clothes *'cling to her'*. Not only do they fit her, they will not let go of her. There is the suggestion they make her more attractive. It may mean she feels more desirable – she was *'aflame'*.

Q How does her school friend respond to her salwar kameez? How do you think she feels about this?

PRACTICE

Complete this chart by making notes on what you learn about the different cultures and how the poet feels about them:

The culture	What you learn about the culture from the poem	How the poet feels about the culture
Her native culture – Pakistan		
Her adopted culture – England		

People and places
'Blessing' by Imtiaz Dharker and 'Nothing's changed' by Tatamkhulu Afrika

THE BARE BONES

➤ It is important to recognise the effect of the environment on people's lives.

➤ An environment can be a natural one or it can be formed by social or political influences.

A 'Blessing' by Imtiaz Dharker

KEY FACT

A person's environment can be religious.

1 In 'Blessing', the coming of rain is viewed as god-given.

- The subject of this poem is water. The poet considers it both a necessity and something of value. He calls it a blessing, suggesting it is god-given.
- The poem starts and ends with the effect of water. The poem shows how the people are made physically aware of the water's coming (*'drip and splash'*). The flow has produced a *'roar of tongues'* – it is seen as a gift from God.
- When the early Christians spoke in many tongues, it was seen as a sign that the Holy Spirit had descended on them. This had given the people inspiration, as the coming of water gives hope to the people of the village.

2 The environment can be our physical surroundings.

- These people live in rough homes on the edge of the city. At first, they are nowhere to be seen. They appear only with the sudden rush of water.
- Notice that they are not described as individuals. They are seen impersonally as *'every man woman child'*. Their individuality is lost in the *'congregation'* and the focus is kept on the rain.

KEY FACT

The environment can be experienced through the language.

1 Sound is used to convey the coming of rain.

- To convey the water shortage, the poet uses a simile: skin *'cracks like a pod'*. The effect of the drought is conveyed by the noise the crack makes in the silence. He describes rain falling (*'drip, splash, echo'*) as sound, not something to feel.
- The noise in the mug is the voice of a kindly god, which links with the idea that water is a blessing from God.

2 Adjectives are used to carry meaning.

- When the water appears, it is accompanied by the phrase *'liquid sun'*. The word *'liquid'* is normally used to describe water. Here, it has been transferred from 'water' to 'sunlight'. This technique compresses two different ideas into one and makes the writing more powerful.
- When the gift has been bestowed, the water flows over *'their small bones'*. The adjective *'small'* may mean that the bones are literally small and belong to young children. It also implies, however, that the people have not grown as tall as they might, because of the chronic lack of water.

Q Pick out and list examples of noise. How do they emphasise the people's needs?

B *Nothing's changed* by Tatamkhulu Afrika

Remember
The man's anger reminds him of how he felt when he was a boy.

Q What do *'flaring', 'guard'* and *'crushed'* tell you about how the poet feels towards this development?

Q What do the phrases *'I back from the glass'* and *'shiver down the glass'* tell you about the man's reaction to this new development?

Environment can be social or political.

1 The place where we live can affect the way we react.

- In **stanza one**, the environment is harsh (*'hard stones'*) and neglected (*'weeds'*). But the weeds are *'amiable'* (friendly, easy to get on with), suggesting the narrator's feelings about the place.

- **Stanza two** shows that he has an instinctive feel for the land (*'my feet know'*). His reactions produce a shift in tone (*'anger of my eyes'*). The poet directs the reader's attention to the object of his anger – a new up-market inn.

2 Politics affect the way we react to events.

- The poem is set in a country that used to operate an apartheid system, where Blacks were not allowed to mix with Whites. Although the system no longer exists, there is still discrimination. The inn, though *'no sign says it is'*, is for Whites only. The Blacks eat down the road in the *'working man's café'.*

- In the **final stanza**, the man leaves a *'small mean O'* on the window. He has become like a boy again. He feels small against the size of this development. His anger makes him want to destroy it.

- The separation of the two cultural groups, Blacks and Whites, is presented through the symbol of glass. The phrase *'Brash with glass'* suggests the new development does not fit in with the natural environment. It is garish and unfriendly. The Port Jackson trees are also out of place. They are imported.

- *'I press my nose/to the clear panes'*: this indicates that the man has been excluded from the new building; the glass is a barrier, through which he can see what is happening on the other side.

PRACTICE

Reread lines 25–40 of 'Nothing's changed'. What contrasting pictures are you given of the White and the Black cultures? How are you shown the unfairness of this in the poem as a whole?

THE BARE BONES

➤ Shakespeare uses images of <u>light</u> and <u>dark</u> to highlight the conflict between the Capulets and the Montagues.

➤ In order to appreciate the language, it helps to understand how paradoxes are used.

A Contrasting images

KEY FACT

Language is used to express the struggle between two warring families.

1 Contrasting symbols are used to highlight the struggle.

Romeo and Juliet is a play of conflict between two warring families, the Capulets and the Montagues. Shakespeare highlights this conflict with contrasting images of **light** and **dark**. A brainstorm on images of light and dark shows what they might represent in the play.

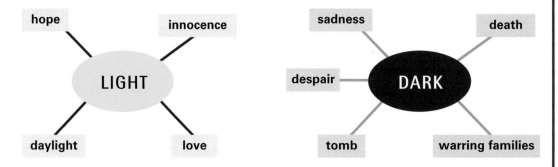

Q. Add some suggestions of your own to this brainstorm.

Remember
Look for images that reflect hope and despair.

2 Contrasts are used within images to emphasise this sense of conflict.

- When Juliet describes her lover in Act III, scene ii, she says:

    'Come, night; come Romeo; come, thou day in night;
    For thou wilt lie upon the wings of night
    Whiter than new snow on a raven's back.' (lines 17–20)

- Romeo is seen as being *'whiter than new snow on a raven's back'*. The new snow represents the innocence of young love. The choice of a black bird, the raven, might suggest the darkness of night, fear, uncertainty or depression caused by parental opposition. The dark image hints at the tragic ending that is to follow.

- Look at the following examples of images of light and dark in Act II, scene ii:

    'The brightness of her cheeks would shame those stars' (line 19)

    'Thou know'st the mask of night is on my face' (line 89)

Remember
Find and explain the contrast within an image.

Notice the contrast between the *'brightness of cheeks'* and the *'mask of night'*. The brightness suggests her youthful innocence. The *'mask of night'* symbolises the darker forces at work in the play. Notice that a mask is used to conceal (in this case, the darker forces). By contrast, Juliet's innocence is there for all to see in her face.

B The use of paradox

Paradoxes are used to create a sense of confusion.

- In Act 1, scene i, Romeo is confused. He is being questioned by Benvolio about being in love and notices that a fight has taken place. Romeo's speech echoes his confusion:

  'Here's much to do with hate, but more with love:
  Why then, O <u>brawling love</u>, O <u>loving hate</u>,
  O any thing of nothing first create!
  O <u>heavy lightness, serious vanity</u>,
  Misshapen chaos of well-seeming forms,
  <u>Feather of lead, bright smoke, cold fire, sick health</u>,
  <u>Still-waking sleep</u>, that is not what it is!' (lines 166–172)

- In these lines, Shakespeare makes extensive use of paradox, as you can see from the underlining. The paradox of *'brawling love'* is a hint at what is to come later. Romeo falls in love with a Capulet, Juliet, but, because he is a Montague and a loyal friend to Mercutio, he kills Tybalt, Juliet's cousin.

- Everything Romeo sees around him seems contradictory. Even fire to him seems cold. The use of paradox is very effective here, allowing Romeo to reveal his confused feelings to the audience. Remember, at the time, he believes himself to be in love with Rosaline. The audience can find a new truth about the play. Love is blind, as we say, and full of confusion.

Remember
A paradox is an apparent contradiction that serves to reveal a new truth.

Remember
Look for contradictions in the text and work out what is suggested by them.

PRACTICE

1 Explain the contradictions in the following phrases:

brawling love	love is not usually linked with fighting
loving hate	
heavy lightness	
serious vanity	
feather of lead	
bright smoke	
cold fire	
sick health	
still-waking sleep	

2 Consider these images from Act II, scene iii:
- *'the white wonder of Juliet's hand'*
- *'Now I have stained the childhood of our joy'*
- *'to blaze your marriage'.*

  Show what they symbolise in the play.

Empathy in drama
Romeo and Juliet, Act III, scene v

THE BARE BONES

➤ To understand drama, it is necessary to empathise with a character and that character's situation.

➤ To help the audience empathise, Shakespeare uses a range of dramatic features.

A Dramatic features

KEY FACT

In order to empathise with characters and their situation, consider a range of dramatic features.

1 Look at the dramatic situation of 'Romeo and Juliet'.
At the start of the scene, Juliet is trying to persuade Romeo to stay. He says he must go or else he will be captured and put to death. They are in a desperate situation. Romeo is so desperate his thoughts turn to death.

> *'let me be put to death'* (line 17)
> *'Come, death and welcome'* (line 24)

Once Juliet realises the danger he is in, she too urges him to go:

> *'O now be gone, more light and light it grows.'*

2 The speed of events increases the audience's understanding of the characters' predicament.
When the nurse announces the arrival of Lady Capulet, notice how the **speed** of events quickens. **Suddenly**, the lovers are concerned about when and if they will meet again. The knowledge that Juliet's mother is coming means things have to be rushed. This **sense of urgency** makes the audience more anxious about the lovers' fate, particularly when Lady Capulet calls out before entering.

3 The dramatic tension is increased through misunderstanding.
Lady Capulet misunderstands Juliet's reaction. The misunderstanding increases because Juliet cannot say what she really thinks. When Lady Capulet calls Romeo *'villain'*, Juliet can speak her true feelings only as an aside.

There is a dramatic change in mood when Lady Capulet switches the topic of conversation to marriage:

> *'But now I'll tell thee joyful tidings, girl.'*

Q How does Juliet react when she hears her mother's *'joyful tidings'?*

B Use of language

> In order to empathise with character and situation, you need to understand the way in which language is used.

1 The poetic images help the audience to appreciate the dramatic predicament.

The way in which Romeo and Juliet see their own predicament helps the audience to appreciate their feelings and the nature of their tragedy.

Juliet pleads with Romeo to stay:

> *'It is the lark that sings so out of tune'* (line 27).

The lark singing out of tune is a symbol of the lack of harmony in Verona. Juliet emphasises the conflict she is caught up in when she speaks of *'harsh discords'* (line 28).

Romeo is so despondent: *'let me be put to death' (line 17).* He speaks *'As one dead in the bottom of a tomb'.*

2 The tone and shifts in tone help the audience to understand how Juliet is feeling.

Consider Juliet's different reactions in this scene:

'Madam, in happy time, what day is that?' (line 115) shows Juliet pretending that she doesn't know what is really going on.

'He shall not make me there a joyful bride.' (line 119) When Juliet is told she is to marry the Count Paris, she says what she really thinks.

'I swear/It shall be Romeo' (lines 125–6) shows she cannot hold back her true feelings any longer.

'Proud can I never be of what I hate.' (line 151) When Capulet criticises Juliet for her ungrateful attitude, she decides to go on the attack by throwing his words (*'Is she not proud?'*) back at him.

'make the bridal bed
In that dim monument where Tybalt lies' (lines 210–11). When Juliet turns to her mother for help, her words predict her own tragic end.

'Well, thou hast comforted me much' (line 242). Juliet's ironic response to the Nurse shows how deeply she is hurt by her old friend's lack of support.

Through these shifts in tone, the audience can experience for themselves the changing emotions felt by Juliet. Their understanding of her character and her situation is enhanced.

PRACTICE

1 Show how Shakespeare helps the audience to understand Romeo's position in Act II, scene ii.

2 Show how Shakespeare involves the audience in Juliet's situation in Act III, scene iii.

Comedy in tragedy
Romeo and Juliet - a study of three characters

THE BARE BONES

➤ Although a tragedy, the play contains several unexpected comic moments.

➤ Comic moments provide light relief and allow the audience to keep a balanced view of the tragedy.

➤ The comedy in the play rests mainly on three characters.

A The Nurse

KEY FACT

The Nurse expresses her comedy through her relationship with Juliet.

Remember
Be aware of the reactions of others to the Nurse.

1 The Nurse embarrasses Juliet to comic effect.
- Look at Act I, scene iii (lines 11–54), where the Nurse is describing events when Juliet was a child – a teenager is having her early embarrassments exposed. The audience is amused because most of them have experienced it for themselves.
- When the question of Juliet's age is brought up, the Nurse cannot resist making a joke of it, by referring to the number of teeth in her mouth:

  'And yet, to my teen, be it spoken, I have but four' (lines 13–14).

- There is no need to explain the pun on *'fourteen'*. Simply show **how** it is used to amuse the audience.

2 The reactions of others to the Nurse increase the comic effect.
- Juliet is annoyed by the Nurse's ramblings and Lady Capulet is irritated by her. Look at the speech beginning *'Marry, that 'marry' is the very theme . . .'* (lines 53–5) and notice how Shakespeare brings out their irritable feelings here.
- The Nurse takes an age to get to the point and uses delaying tactics. Juliet and Lady Capulet are frustrated by her asides and repetitions.

Q Make a note of some of the asides and repetitions to be found in lines 13–40.

3 The memories of the Nurse amuse the audience.
The Nurse makes bawdy comments such as: *'thou wilt fall backward when thou hast more wit'* (Act I, scene iii, lines 36–7). These comments introduce a note of realism into a play about romantic love.

B Mercutio

KEY FACT

Mercutio uses comedy to express his feelings about others.

Q How does Romeo sum up Mercutio later in this scene?

1 His wit is enjoyable but it has a sharp edge to it.
In Act II, scene iv (line 72), Mercutio remarks *'wit is a very bitter sweeting'*. In his exchanges with the Nurse in Act II, scene v (lines 90–125), he compares her bulk to a sail. He trades bawdy jokes with her, such as: *'for the bawdy hand of the dial is now upon the prick of noon'* (line 101). He insults her, calling her *'ancient lady'.*

B

Q What are the words Mercutio and Romeo play on in lines 43–89? What are the different meanings placed on these words by the two men?

2 <u>Mercutio uses his wit against his enemies.</u>
- Mercutio expresses his feelings about Tybalt:

   'he is the courageous captain of compliments: he fights as you sing . . . the very butcher of a silk button' (Act II, scene iv, lines 18–22).

- The sneering alliteration of *'courageous captain'* shows the contempt he has for him. He appears to build up Tybalt's reputation as a fierce fighter (*'butcher'*), but then destroys this reputation by saying he chooses easy targets (*'silk button'*).

3 <u>Mercutio loves to trade witty remarks with his friends.</u>
   In the section, lines 43–89, starting: *'Good morrow to you both? What counterfeit did I give you?'*, notice the delight with which he and Romeo trade puns

C *Friar Lawrence*

EY FACT

Friar Lawrence has a comic side to him.

1 <u>The tone of Friar Lawrence's humour is gentle.</u>
   In Act II, scene iii (lines 33–88), you will find examples of the Friar's gentle playfulness. In his greeting, notice how he shows an amused understanding of young people.

Remember
Emphasise the tone of the Friar's humour.

2 <u>The Friar uses innuendo to make his points.</u>
   The Friar suggests that Romeo has been making love to Rosaline. He finds it surprising that a young man can be out of bed so early; he must be ill, or he hasn't been to bed!

Remember
Comic figures are often critical of tragic characters.

3 <u>The Friar criticises through gentle mockery.</u>
   The Friar fondly mocks Romeo. He tells him: *'Riddling confession finds but riddling shift'* (line 59), meaning that if he can't speak plainly, he won't get a straight answer.

   He shows surprise that Romeo now loves Juliet and not Rosaline, mocking the inconstancy of youth by speaking of *'the stain . . . of an old tear'* (lines 78–9) on Romeo's face. He compares Romeo's love for Rosaline to an immature child who cannot spell. Romeo knows he is being mocked, pleading: *'I pray thee, chide not'* (line 89).

PRACTICE

Show how Shakespeare makes the Nurse a comic character in Act III, scene ii.

To do this comment on the use of:
- repetition
- asides
- delay
- puns
- innuendo.

Dramatic devices
Romeo and Juliet – an analysis of Act I, scene v

THE BARE BONES

➤ Drama is to be found in conflict.

➤ The sense of drama is emphasised by the language used.

A Conflict in the play

Remember
Be aware of the language of conflict used in verbal exchanges.

Drama is found in conflict, and conflict in the play is found in:

1 physical struggle that ends in death

2 physical objects that act as agents of conflict and tragedy. In Romeo and Juliet they are such things as the phial of poison and Romeo's dagger

3 the language of conflict to be found in the way the characters speak

4 the tone, mood or atmosphere and the ways in which they change.

B Analysing a scene

1 **Read the scene very carefully.**
   Close reading of the text is essential. If necessary, read the scene through several times. Read the scene with the question you are answering firmly in your mind. As you go through the text, highlight the words and phrases that are relevant to your answer.

2 **Break the scene down into smaller, separate sections.**
   You will find that most scenes can be broken down into miniature scenes, each of which involves a smaller number of characters than appears in the scene as a whole. In Act I, scene v, you could find eight sections involving these characters:

- the servants
- Capulet, Second Capulet, Juliet and the Guests and Maskers
- Romeo and servant
- Tybalt and Capulet
- Romeo and Juliet and the Nurse
- Romeo and Benvolio
- Romeo, Benvolio and Capulet
- Juliet and Nurse.

Q Trace and identify the different mood changes in Act I, scene v.

3 **Identify the mood of each section.**
   You will find the scene opens with the anxiety of the servants and the anger of Tybalt. You will discover that the mood changes from section to section. This will help you to understand the emotional shifts throughout the scene.

Remember
Write about the effects of changes of mood on the audience.

B

4 <u>Comment on the physical elements in the scene.</u>

Notice how the music contributes to the atmosphere of the scene. Show how the masks add uncertainty and a feeling of tension to the scene.

5 <u>Comment on the language used.</u>

For example, in lines 59–60, Tybalt says:

'Now by the stock and honour of my kin,
to strike him dead I hold it not a sin.'

Here, Tybalt gives two reasons for killing Romeo. Firstly, in killing him, he would be upholding the family name (*'honour'*). It is, he says, what his family has been bred for (*'stock'*). He thinks it almost a religious duty (*'I hold it not a sin'*). By doing this, you are explaining the source of dramatic tension. You are showing how the audience is made aware of the conflict to come.

PRACTICE

Consider each of the following key sections from Act I, scene v. Show which dramatic elements each contains.

1 FIRST SERVANT. Away with the joint-stools, remove the court-cupboard, look to the plate. Good thou, save me a piece of marchpane;

2 CAPULET. Welcome, gentlemen! I have seen the day
That I have worn a visor and could tell
A whispering tale in a fair lady's ear,
Such as would please: 'tis gone, 'tis gone 'tis gone.

3 ROMEO. O she doth teach the torches to burn bright
It seems she hangs upon the cheek of night
Like a rich jewel in an Ethiop's ear.

4 TYBALT. This by his voice, should be a Montague.
Fetch me my rapier, boy. What dares the slave,
Come hither covered with an antic face.

5 ROMEO. If I profane with my unworthiest hand
This holy shrine, the gentle sin is this:
My lips two blushing pilgrims ready stand
To smooth that rough touch with a tender kiss.

JULIET. Good pilgrim you do wrong your hand too much
Which mannerly devotion shows in this;
For saints have hands that pilgrims' hands do touch
And palm to palm is holy palmers' kiss.

6 NURSE. I nursed her daughter, that you talk'd withal;
I tell you, he that can lay hold of her
Shall have the chinks.

7 BENVOLIO. Away be gone; the sport is at the best.

ROMEO. Ay, so I fear; the more is my unrest.

8 JULIET. Go, ask his name: if he be married,
My grave is like to be my wedding bed.

Non-fiction texts

THE BARE BONES

➤ Non-fiction texts are texts that are not poems, stories, novels or plays.
➤ They include newspapers, magazine articles, information leaflets, advertisements, biographies and autobiographies, letters and diaries, travel writing and reference books.
➤ They are written to inform, to persuade, to give advice or to describe.

A What skills do I need?

You are expected to:

1 extract information from texts

2 distinguish between fact and opinion

3 follow and explain the writer's arguments

4 select material according to purpose

5 write about the way in which the information is presented

6 consider how effectively the information is presented

B Reading in the exam

KEY FACT

To do well in exams, you need to be a very efficient reader.

Follow these steps:

1 The first thing to read in an examination is the question or task set, so you know what you're looking for when you read the text.

2 Now read the text once, so you have a general idea of what it contains. Don't worry if you do not understand or remember everything the first time you read it.

3 The second time you read the text, you'll be reading it to look for a particular piece of information needed to answer a question. This is known as scanning

KEY FACT

You'll find it helpful to underline the relevant parts of a text to help you answer an exam question.

Refer to the text frequently to support your answers. You must give as much evidence of your reading as you can.

c Becoming familiar with non-fiction texts

- Non-fiction texts are all around us in the form of adverts, leaflets, information sheets, newpapers, junk mail and many more items.

- Get familiar with this type of text by reading some of the non-fiction texts that you see around you. Try to work out what techniques their writers have used to get their information across in an interesting and appealing way.

PRACTICE

Study these texts and work out why they were written and in what sort of publication they would appear.

B

Castle: a large fortified building. The name comes form the Latin word *castellum,* which means a small fortified place. Castles were built to keep out invaders. Throughout history, castles have undergone many changes to adapt to changes in weapons and defence techniques. Castles in the middle ages were built on mounds of earth surrounded by a wooden fence. This was known as a motte-and-bailey castle. This type of castle was later built in stone. The White Tower of London is one of the simplest stone castles, known as a keep or donjon. Later, stone castles became more sophisticated in design. Castles such as Caernafon Castle in Wales have battlemented towers and outer walls known as curtain walls.

A

How to Vote

This leaflet tells you how you can still vote even if you are unable to go to your polling station on election day. Providing there is a good reason why you cannot vote in person, you can apply to vote by post or proxy.
(A proxy is someone who votes on your behalf.)

For example:
- if you will be away on holiday (in the UK or abroad)
- if your work takes you away from home
- if you are ill or in hospital.

Some people qualify to vote by post or proxy for a longer period of time, not just at one particular election.

C

YOUR HEALTH

with Dr Kay Hadley

• • • • • • • • • • • • • • • • • • • •

How can I heal all my burns?

Q I cook a lot and am prone to small burns on my hands and wrists. Is there any way that I can soothe these naturally and, perhaps, get them to heal more quickly? *J. Smith, London.*

A The most important thing after you have burnt yourself is to run cold water over the burn. This takes much of the heat out of it and helps to limit its severity. For maximum benefit, keep the burn under cold running water for several minutes and apply ice, too.
While minor burns can be treated at home, large or severe injuries should be looked at by a doctor, just in case you need medical treatment.
Pure essential oil of lavender can be soothing. Apply it several times a day while the burn is healing. This will help it heal quickly with the minimum scarring.

THE BARE BONES

➤ To extract information quickly and efficiently, use reading techniques known as <u>skimming</u> and <u>scanning</u>.

➤ <u>Skimming</u> a text means reading it quickly to get the main points.

➤ <u>Scanning</u> a text means reading a text to look out for particular details or information.

A Extracting information

Remember
- Skim
- Scan
- Highlight
- Write answer

1 Skim read the questions first, so you know what you are looking for. If you do this, you will get an idea of the main points of the text before you even read it.

2 Skim read the whole text once to work out what it is about and what the main points are. Don't worry if you don't remember details from the text at this stage.

3 When you are ready to answer the questions, underline the key words in each one.
For example:
Name <u>four</u> ways in which <u>students</u> are helped to find <u>part-time jobs</u>.

4 Now scan the text, looking out for the information you have highlighted in the question. Ignore the rest of the text and only concentrate on looking for what you need to answer a particular question.

5 When you have found the information, underline it on the text.

6 Use this information to answer the question.

7 Keep your information short – do not copy out whole chunks of text.

B Collating information

KEY FACT

Exam questions often ask you to combine information that you have extracted from different texts. This is known as <u>collating</u> information.

- When you are collating information, you use the same **skimming and scanning techniques** that you used for extracting information.
- Use a **highlighter** to underline points on **both** texts. If you do this, you will be able to check that you have included information from both texts.

B

Remember

- Make sure you include the exact number of points that the question asks for.

- Underline key words in the question.

Just £8 makes the difference between life and death

- £8 goes towards first aid and essential medication given to a rescued animal.

- £8 will help the RSPCA build and run animal shelters where abandoned animals find safety; where the beaten and tortured receive veterinary care; and where the neglected and ignored find love.

- £8 helps to pay the cost of starting a new RSPCA inspector's training.

WILD REFUGE

The more we encroach on nature, the more work we create for wildlife sanctuaries. Chris Hulme reports.

We Britons are proud of our reputation as animal lovers. In every town and city, there are countless people concerned about the welfare of creatures great and small. Unfortunately, that's not the whole story. The reality of life in any industrial country is that wildlife usually comes off second best in encounters with humans. Cars, pollution, building projects and downright cruelty all regularly claim casualties.

The RSPCA is doing what it can to redress the balance. The society has three specialist wildlife hospitals which treat injured or orphaned animals, always with the objective of returning them to their natural habitat.

C Putting information into your own words

Sometimes exam questions ask you to extract information and then put it into your own words. This is known as using the technique of <u>reorganisation</u>.

- To reorganise information, follow the steps as in Section A. Highlight the key point in the question, and then scan the text to find the appropriate information.

- Next, instead of listing the highlighted information, **write your own version**.

PRACTICE

You will risk losing marks if you do not use your own words.

Read the two texts below. **Explain in your own words** what problems face these two species. Refer to both texts in your answer.

Adopt a dolphin

Meet Sundance. He pursues a life of fun, friendship and freedom off the coast of the Moray Firth in Scotland. A lifestyle which may not be sustainable for much longer. Pollution, over-fishing, capture and drowning in fishing nets are daily threats to dolphins like Sundance.

ADOPT A RHINO

Kinyanju is a black rhino. Not so long ago – only as far back as the seventies – he would have been one of 6000 in Africa. Now a monstrous trade has decimated these numbers. A staggering 95% of black rhinos have been cold-bloodedly butchered for their horns.

Today, Kinyanju is one of only 434 of these magnificent beasts left alive in Kenya.

THE BARE BONES
> <u>Facts</u> can be proved.
> <u>Opinions</u> are statements of belief.

A How to spot facts and opinions

KEY FACT

Remember
Facts often contain numbers.

Facts are supported by evidence.

For example:

- In AD 79, the volcano Mount Vesuvius erupted.

  This figure could be **checked** *in history books.*

- Some of the world's highest volcanoes are in the Andes in South America.

  This fact could be **checked** *in geography books.*

KEY FACT

Opinions are what people <u>believe</u> or <u>think</u> – they are personal.

For example:
Many people believe dogs are man's best friend.

B Telling the difference

Sometimes it is not easy to tell the difference between facts and opinions.

This is a **fact** that could be proved by visiting or telephoning the shop.

The use of the number might make you think this is a fact. But not everyone would consider the offers to be fantastic. This is an opinion.

UP TO **£100** free frozen food on selected models!

5 FANTASTIC OFFERS!

C Looking at the language of opinions

Advertisers often use language emotively to appeal to the feelings or emotions of readers. Language used emotively is a good clue to look for when you are trying to spot opinions.

Q Look at this extract and find two examples of words and phrases that are used emotively.

Easy pickings on the street

As a part of our car tests we check the security of doors, windows, boot or tailgate, bonnet, glovebox, steering-column lock, petrol-filler lock and sunroof.

Here we tell you what we've found. It adds up to a sorry picture for car owners and a disgraceful one for car-makers.

C

Another way to spot an opinion is to look for the words that introduce it.

These words are often used to introduce an opinion:

appear   suggest   may   might   should   could   would

These words all suggest **possibilities** rather than something that is definite and can be proved like a fact.

Look out for these words as you pick out the **opinions** from this extract:

Buying a car is, for many people, the second most costly purchase they make in their life – second only to buying their own home. And yet car-makers seem to put car security pretty low on their list of priorities.

We can't publicly blow the whistle on the specific design weaknesses we find in doors and locks, for fear of worsening the crime rate. But the makers know the problems as well as we do. They should be making doors more secure, protecting the ignition system and fitting an alarm system as standard (or, at least, offering it as an option). The car-makers must take more action to combat the sky-high car crime figures.

Q Which is a fact and which is an opinion?

- For just £1 a week you can sponsor an abandoned dog like me today.
- Now isn't that a pound well spent?

PRACTICE

Car Alarms

How they raise the alarm
The alarms set off either the car's horn or their own sounder – a horn or siren. Using the car's horn might be a bit of a risk if the thief is familiar with the car – he could open the bonnet and cut the horn connections. A siren is a distinctive sound – people nearby might take notice more quickly. Flashing headlights and indicators, are likely to raise eyebrows, especially at night.

Does it immobilise the car?
Many alarms also knock out the car's ignition. This is obviously a worthwhile protection – if a thief knocks out the horn he may still be unable to drive off.

What triggers the alarm?
Alarms can be triggered by vibrations made by a thief before the door is opened, a door being opened, or by something inside (the thief's movement, or by the engine being started, for example). The sooner the alarm goes off, the better.

How persistent is the alarm?
Many of the alarms go off only for a limited time after some sort of disturbance – sensible as it

avoids too much unnecessary rumpus. Most importantly, all the vibration alarms stopped after a while if accidentally triggered off. But a cut-off could be bad if it left the car exposed after the thief's initial attack – some alarms stopped even though the door was still open.

Security against alarm being switched off
The alarm's switch is a weak point. Perhaps the weakest is a key switch outside the car that can be picked easily. Many alarms are worked by a flick switch inside – totally vulnerable once found, though the thief would have to brazen out the noise while looking.

How convenient?
Simple flick switches are quite convenient. A few systems worked with the car's ignition switch – even more convenient.

False alarming?
A car alarm that goes off unnecessarily, because the car is buffeted by gusts of wind, say, can drive people nearby to distraction. Some alarms were more prone to accidental triggering than others.

1 The extract above contains both facts and opinions. Find five examples of each.

2 Write them down in two separate lists headed FACT and OPINION

Following an argument

THE BARE BONES

➤ Following an argument means understanding and explaining the points of view presented in a text.

➤ Following an argument is a very important skill when answering exam questions.

A   How to follow an argument

KEY FACT

When presenting their argument or point of view, writers use both <u>facts</u> and <u>opinions</u>.

For example:
One writer might argue that the minimum age for legally buying fireworks should be raised due to an increasing number of firework accidents among young people. To make this argument, the writer might include **facts** about the dangers of fireworks, as well as his own **opinion** of the irresponsible behaviour of young people.

B   How to spot the development of an argument

1 Read the whole passage.

2 Underline the key words and phrases that reveal the writer's opinion.

3 Look out for facts that support this opinion.

4 Work out the different stages of the argument. Does the writer's opinion change throughout the text?

- Read through the article below, which presents one woman's view about putting her mother into a residential home for old people.

- In the first part, she reveals the **difficulties** she has in caring for her mother and her **worries** about putting her into a home.

Q Underline the words and phrases that reveal these difficulties and problems.

Is it fair to put Mum in a home?

Mum is 88, and she'd lived in West London for 53 years before she had a fall in April this year and was taken into hospital. I'd always worried that if she needed more care, I couldn't cope at home. She needs lots of help, but wouldn't want me to give up my career. It would be impossible for her to live with us – our house is too small.

But all the guilt and the social pressures are horrendous. A lot of people are shocked that I could even think about putting my mother in a home.

Mum hates hospitals, and her mental state was deteriorating when she first went in. She had another fall in hospital, but then she was transferred to a terrific rehabilitation ward.

The social workers there said Mum's needs would be assessed to see what sort of care she required. I was scared she'd need nursing care – a lot of people in nursing homes are very confused, and I was worried that Mum would be put in a room full of mad people.

B

Q Can you spot the sentence that marks the turning point in the writer's argument?

- Now read the rest of the article and list the positive results of putting her mother in a home.

> I started looking at homes, and the one I'm hoping Mum will go to looks excellent. We're still waiting for the final assessment and for the council to agree that this particular home is right for Mum.
>
> Before she had her fall I knew she needed help, but I couldn't persuade her to take it. Now I know she'll be well cared for, her meals will be cooked for her and she'll have people around her, and we've actually become closer as a result of her fall.

- In the next example – a report from the *Guardian* newspaper – the writer comments on various points of view related to the changing world.

Remember
- Read the questions first and underline key words – look for these words in the article.
- Always answer in your own words and back up your answer with evidence from the article.

═══════════════════════════════════

Queen, 71, bemoans trials of modern life

Jamie Wilson on varied reactions to the monarch's reflections

She may have her own internet site, and was jetting around the world before most people had ever been airborne, but yesterday the Queen confessed that she found it hard to keep up with the modern world.

The 71-year-old monarch, who is in Pakistan on the second day of her state visit, told the country's parliament: "I sometimes sense that the world is changing almost too fast for its inhabitants, at least for us older ones."

Her comments drew support from a number of her more elderly subjects. Veteran writer and broadcaster Ludovic Kennedy said he agreed entirely: "What she has said is absolutely right. For old dogs like us, new tricks are simply unacceptable."

Mr Kennedy, 77, continued: "The world is changing so fast we just can't keep pace with it.

"That is something older people have to accept."

Romantic novelist Dame Barbara Cartland, 95, echoed the Queen's sentiments, saying: "The world is changing too fast. The Queen is right, we need to get back to the way we were in the past.

"We need to get back to a previous age, where men behaved like gentlemen and women were women and not so busy building their careers. I think that is what

the Queen was trying to say and I agree with her."

However, Tony Benn, the 72-year-old Labour MP, felt one change was long overdue.

"The one thing that has not changed in my lifetime is the monarchy. If we could move into the next century with an elected head of state I would feel optimistic," he said.

But it was not all pessimism at the fast rate of progress. Betty Felsted from St Albans, a 70-year-old member of the Women's League of Health and Beauty, said that old people were sometimes blinded by science but that should not stop them from trying to keep up. "Just before I retired I learned how to use a word processor and I have no problem with video recorders or washing machines: I just read the instructions and get on with it.

"I always have a go at anything that comes along."

But Age Concern spokesman Margaret McLellan was sympathetic to the Queen's remarks, saying: "Many elderly people will feel the same way as the Queen.

"Feeling too old to catch up with the modern world can begin when people are as young as 40 or 50, and it is a feeling which gets worse as people get older."

PRACTICE

1 What point is the Queen making about modern life?

2 How does Ludovic Kennedy support and extend the Queen's point of view?

3 Look again at Barbara Cartland's views on the changing world. In what ways are her arguments different from those of Ludovic Kennedy?

4 What does Tony Benn's contribution add to the argument?

5 In what way do Betty Felsted's arguments disagree with some of the previous statements?

6 Out of all the views presented in this article, which is the closest to the views of the Queen? Explain why.

THE BARE BONES

➤ Texts differ according to their <u>purpose</u> and <u>intended audience</u>.

A Identifying the purpose of a text

Q Can you think of two reasons why a newspaper article might be written?

The purpose of a text is the reason why it was written. You need to ask yourself: **Why** was it written? Was it written to:

- inform
- entertain
- explain
- advise
- instruct
- persuade
- for some other reason?

Sometimes texts can be written for more than one purpose. For example, an advertisement can be written to inform and persuade.

KEY FACT

You can work out the purpose of a text by studying its <u>features</u>.

- Look closely at this text and place the features from the list next to the appropriate arrows:

IMPORTANT SAFEGUARDS

When using electrical appliances, basic safety precautions should always be followed, including the following:

1. Read all instructions.
2. Do not touch hot surfaces.
3. To protect against electric shock do not immerse cord or plugs in water or other liquids.
4. Do not insert metal objects, knives, forks or similar implements into the bread slot.

Features

- begins with statement of what is to be achieved
- short, clear sentences
- numbered lists to sequence writing
- imperatives

- These features tell you that this is a **set of instructions**
- Read the text below, which has been written **to persuade**

now she's old enough to look after her own smile – what about yours?

RETURN TO NURSING Full or part-time flexible hours
Giving up a few years to look after a child has its own special rewards. But when they no longer need all of your time, returning to work can be a daunting prospect. Whatever your reason for taking time out, don't worry – your nursing skills are always valuable, whether they were learned 10 months or 10 years ago. If you've had a break from nursing, for however long, we can offer you one of the best ways to get back in.

Features

- begins with an opening statement
- finishes with a summary or repetition of the opening statement
- refers to the reader personally
- uses emotive language to appeal to feelings of readers

Q Can you find examples in the text of each of these features?

B Identifying the audience

Q What clues tell you this text was written for young people?

Remember
When working out the audience for a text, look at the subject matter. What is it about?
Look at the vocabulary. Who would use these sorts of words?
What sorts of illustrations are used?

To identify the audience for a text, you need to ask yourself:

Who was it written for? Was it written for an adult, teenager or child, or a combination of these? Was it written for someone with a particular interest?

Look at this text:

What Can I do About Having Parents?

Well, the first thing I would say is this:
don't panic!
As I mentioned previously, everyone has at some point had parents. So, you're not alone. Although I realise it can seem that way. It can seem very traumatic.

Look at this text. Who is the audience and how can you tell?

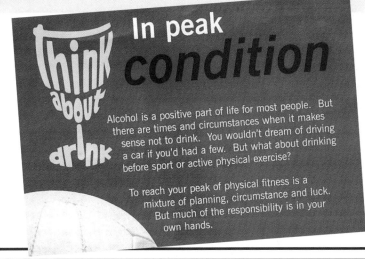

In peak condition

think about drink

Alcohol is a positive part of life for most people. But there are times and circumstances when it makes sense not to drink. You wouldn't dream of driving a car if you'd had a few. But what about drinking before sport or active physical exercise?

To reach your peak of physical fitness is a mixture of planning, circumstance and luck. But much of the responsibility is in your own hands.

PRACTICE

What is the purpose of this text? How can you tell?

Comment on the subject matter and the language.

What sort of person would read this? Give reasons for your answer.

SAVED
– THANKS TO RSPCA SUPPORTERS

Without the help of animal lovers like you, the RSPCA would be powerless in the war against cruelty and suffering. See for yourself how your donation can help save the lives of animals who have known only fear, pain and suffering.

Locked in a room for weeks without food, 10-year-old retriever Oliver was just half his recommended weight when the RSPCA found him. The vet said Oliver would have been dead within two days if we hadn't rescued him. Now fully recovered thanks to the dedicated care of RSPCA staff, Oliver has finally found the loving home he deserves.

THE BARE BONES

➤ When you evaluate the presentation of a text, you are expected to analyse and explain how the information looks on the page.

KEY FACT

In exam answers, you will be asked to comment on the effect and impact of the <u>appearance of texts</u>. This is known as the <u>layout</u>.

KEY FACT

Layout refers to the type of print used, the pictures or illustrations and the way in which they are used in the text to <u>get the reader's attention</u>.

Remember
In an exam, you could be asked to explain how the layout helps the reader to understand the message of a text.

Here are some of the most commonly used presentational devices.

1 Headlines
The use of **bold lettering**, **capital letters** and an **exclamation mark** makes the headline appear dramatic and eye-catching.

DIRTY WATER KILLS!

Have you got what it takes?

In this headline, the question mark gives you something to think about.

£10 BUYS A CHAIN CUTTER

The pound sign and the number attract your attention here.

❓ What do you notice about the presentation here? How does the presentation help to get the message across?

No time to draw breath?

2 <u>Different sorts of print</u>
Often a text will use different types of print and **font styles** to draw attention to particular points.

The typed letter at the top of the next page opens with a handwritten style. One reason for this is that it makes the appeal **more personal**. It seems as if someone is writing especially to you.

61

action for blind people
....

14-16 Verney Road London SE16 3DZ
Telephone 0171 732 8771 Fax 0171 639 0948

Helping Blind & Partially Sighted people since 1857

Dear friend

I am writing to you this Christmas with a short survey. I hope you will be able to spare just a couple of minutes to complete it. Your response with your views and opinions do matter and will make a vital contribution to our work improving the lives of the blind and partially sighted people all over the country.

3 Logos
Companies and charities use logos as a visual image that you can identify whenever you see them.

4 Charts and diagrams
These are used to present **complex information** in a simple and easy-to-read way.

5 Photographs and illustrations
Visual images have a powerful impact on the reader. We often look at a picture before we read the text. The way pictures are used can set the tone for a text. For example, cartoons can create a jokey effect, while photographs can add a sense of realism.

PRACTICE

1 How many different types of print can you identify?

2 Why do you think the print is of varying sizes?

3 How does the print help to emphasise the message of this text?

4 What impact do you think is made by the pictures?

5 How do the pictures affect the reader's response to this advertisement?

Oxfam
FREEPOST (OF 353)
274 Banbury Road
Oxford OX2 7BR

Help them build a future free from hunger and disease

How does Oxfam make your £2 work so hard?

How can we possibly make just £2 do so much?

The answer lies in the effort, the determination, and the ingenuity of the people we help.

Oxfam doesn't walk into a Third World country with ready-made solutions, or quick-fix answers. We work alongside local people, and help them work out solutions that suit their individual circumstances.

The projects Oxfam supports are always carefully monitored, so that money isn't wasted, and worthwhile lessons can be applied elsewhere.

Oxfam supports 3,000 projects in over 70 countries worldwide.

...for just £2 a month.

**Your £2 a month will help these people in their daily struggle to help themselves.
Please complete the coupon inside.**

THE BARE BONES

➤ Writers match the language they use to their audience and purpose.

➤ The type of language used in a text affects the way the reader receives the message.

➤ Evaluating the language of a text means explaining the impact that the language has on the reader.

Types of language

1 Dramatic or emotive language

Dramatic or emotive language is used to attract the reader's attention, especially in newspaper headlines.

Hospitals face crisis over fall in blood supplies

KEY FACT

Emotive language is language that is intended to arouse strong feelings.

In the example above, the word 'crisis' attracts your attention and encourages you to read the article.

2 Imperatives

KEY FACT

Imperatives are words that give us instructions or orders.

Q What sort of texts do you think are most likely to use imperatives?

Imperatives are used to appeal directly to the reader and to make the message very clear. In this example, the word 'discover' is being used as an imperative.

DISCOVER
Your *FAVOURITE* days out in
CHESHIRE

3 Alliteration

This is where writers use the same letter to start several words in a headline, as in the example. It's a common way of catching the reader's attention.

Ringway rumpus
POLICE were called to Manchester Airport

4 Questions

Questions are used by writers to get the reader involved directly. They have the same effect as the use of imperatives – they make you think the writer is talking to you personally. The article on the next page starts with the question 'How green are you?'.

5 Colloquial language

Colloquial language is informal. It is the language of everyday conversation and is used to make it easy for readers to relate to the text. In the text 'How green are you?', there are several examples of colloquial speech.
This makes the text easy to read and so gets the message across.

Q This article starts with the question 'How green are you?' What effect does this question have on the reader?

How green are you?

Hands up if you have recently done any of the following:

- ■ thrown a glass bottle in the rubbish bin;
- ■ left the tap running while cleaning your teeth;
- ■ poured cooking oil down the drain;
- ■ flushed cotton wool down the loo;
- ■ left the fridge door open while paying the milkman;
- ■ thrown away plastic carriers from the back of a cupboard;
- ■ heated the oven to bake a solitary spud.

Yes, me too. On the other hand, I do recycle bottles, cans and paper, and take clothes to charity shops, so I thought I was doing pretty well, until I started working on this supplement.

Who can put their hand on their heart and honestly say that they always make the greenest decisions about their home?

Q Can you find six examples of colloquial language in the text opposite?

PRACTICE

Friday October 24

Community News

Ninja peril of Black Lake

Dumped terrapins decimate wildlife

An exotic pet which grows from the dimensions of a 50p piece into a plate-sized monster is causing havoc among wildlife after being dumped illegally in a Wilmslow pool.

There are thought to be dozens of American reared terrapins – left-overs of the Ninja Mutant Turtle craze – in Black Lake on Lindow Common.

The 12in-diameter creatures gobble up insects, newts, frogs and even baby water birds. Experts say that unless the terrapins can be curbed local wildlife will be devastated.

The problem began when the terrapins were dumped after they became too big to handle in household aquariums.

The wily reptiles are proving difficult to catch. So far, they have dodged all efforts at trapping.

1 What impression is given of the terrapins in this article?

2 How does the language of the headline and subheading help to emphasise this impression?

3 Choose five words and phrases from the text that you think have been used for dramatic effect. Explain why you think they are dramatic and what readers will think when they read these particular words?

Comparing texts

THE BARE BONES

➤ In exams, you are often asked to write in detail about <u>similarities</u> and <u>differences</u> between two texts.

➤ You will be asked to compare: the content of the texts, the writer's purpose, the way information is presented, the way language is used and the way in which the texts appeal to their audience.

A   The content of a text

KEY FACT

The <u>content</u> means <u>what that text is about</u>. You are expected to write two or three lines to summarise what the text tells you.

Text A

Text B

Discover Hidden Treasure in the Mediterranean

NORTH CYPRUS is a charmed land. A land where you can get away from the crowds and discover miles of deserted beaches, golden sandy beaches. Where you can walk in beautiful mountains, home to rare species of plant and wildlife. A land with a history almost as long as civilisation itself, with a treasure trove of castles, abbeys and palaces, which you can explore at will. An enchanting land where a holiday will feel like a fairy tale.

The Land I Love

One of my earliest memories is walking beside my grandfather in the mountains of Cyprus following our herd of sheep as they climbed higher and higher up the mountain through the **lush green grass** and the **scented wild flowers**. In the middle of the day we used to shelter from the burning sun under large fig trees. If I try hard enough I still can conjure up the taste of their **sweet juicy flesh**.

When we came down from the mountain we used to stop at the well for a drink of the coolest water. In those days Greek and Turkish Cypriots got on well together and we children used to play games in the dusty streets.

On **cold wet days** in the northern industrial town where I now live, my thoughts still wander back to **hot sunny days** in the land I love.

B   The writer's purpose

KEY FACT

The <u>purpose</u> of a text is the <u>reason it was written</u>. Sometimes texts can be written for <u>more than one purpose</u>.

Study this list of purposes for writing:

● to entertain ● to describe ● to argue ● to inform ● to persuade ● to advise.

Q Write one sentence to explain why each of the above texts has been written.

C The way information is presented

When you are asked to **compare** and **contrast** the presentation of a text, look at the following:

- use of headlines and subheadings
- the way paragraphs are arranged
- how the presentation matches the purpose of the text.
- type and size of font
- use of illustration

Q Compare and contrast the way the texts are presented. Explain how the layout of each helps to put across its message.

D The way language is used

Use these **sentence starters** when you are writing to **compare** and **contrast**:

- Both texts . . . ● They are similar because . . . ● Similarly . . . ● In the same way . . .
- They are different because . . . ● On the other hand . . . ● In contrast to . . .

When you **compare** and **contrast** the language of each text, comment on:

- the type of language the writer uses (e.g. is it positive or negative?)

- the reason why the writer has used this sort of language

- the way in which words are placed together; for example, several adjectives used one after the other for maximum impact

- the effect that the language has on the reader, what the reader thinks when reading the text.

Q Compare and contrast the way in which the two texts use language. In particular, refer to the highlighted parts of each text.

E The way in which the texts appeal to their audience

The way in which texts appeal to the reader is often included at the end of an exam answer as a conclusion or summing up of all your points about the texts.

PRACTICE

Look at the two texts on page 64 and answer these questions.

1 Complete these sentences:
- Text A is about . . . It tells the reader . . .
- Text B is about . . . It tells the reader . . .
- Both texts give the reader an impression of Cyprus that is . . .

Note that the comparison of the texts comes in the last sentence and is signalled by the word '*both*'.

2 How are texts A and B similar in the way in which they appeal to readers? Use these **sentence starters** to help you:
- Both texts present a picture of Cyprus that is . . .
- Both texts make the reader want to . . .
- The first text persuades the reader that . . .
- The second text appeals to the reader on a more personal level because . . .

Writing skills

THE BARE BONES

➤ In the exam, you'll be asked to produce writing that argues, persuades or advises, or that explains, informs or describes.

➤ You will be expected to write in a range of different forms, such as letters, leaflets, articles, reports or speeches.

➤ You will be expected to write for a particular audience in a way that gets your message across.

A What skills do I need?

You are expected to:

- plan your work so that the finished piece of writing is well organised

- match your writing to your audience and purpose

- organise your ideas into sentences and paragraphs

- vary the length and style of your sentences

- use a wide range of vocabulary that is suitable for the task

- present your work clearly and neatly using legible handwriting

- use correct punctuation

- spell correctly.

B Planning your writing

KEY FACT

Examiners give credit for work that is well structured and logical, so spend time planning your work before you start writing.

Decide what you are going to say, how you are going to say it and in what order you will present it. Make a simple plan – just a few key words or sentences to help you organise what you want to say.

Remember
Don't forget to match your content, vocabulary and sentence structure to the needs of your audience and the purpose of your task.

C Presentation

Different types of writing need different types of presentation:

- Letters need appropriate beginnings and endings.

- Articles need headlines and subheadings.

- Leaflets need a variety of fonts and different styles of presentation, such as bullet points, to make it easy for the reader to access information quickly.

D Paragraphs

Dividing your ideas into paragraphs helps the reader to follow your argument.

Generally, you should put all your ideas on the same topic in one paragraph. Stop writing every few minutes to read what you have written to see if you need to begin a new paragraph.

E Punctuation

- Punctuation helps the reader to make sense of what is written. Think about where you place commas, full stops, question marks, exclamation marks and ellipses (. . .).
- Go back and check every few sentences to check your punctuation.

F Spelling

Correct spelling is crucial in writing exams. Revise spellings before the exam and make use of spelling rules in your English textbooks.

- Make a note of words that you often get wrong and make a special effort to learn them.
- Pin them up near your desk so you can see them as you do your revision.

G Writing under exam conditions

1 Always spend a few minutes reading the questions. Make your choice carefully so that you know exactly what type of writing is required.

2 Make a plan before you begin writing.

3 Think about each sentence before you write it.

4 Read your work through as you are writing.

PRACTICE

Read this paragraph, which has been written in exam conditions. Can you spot the mistakes?

Ever since I was little I have been intrested in cylcling. My first bike had extra weels to help me balance but I soon graduatd to a bmx I used to where bald patches in the lawn doing my stunts.

Writing for a specific purpose

THE BARE BONES

➤ The <u>purpose</u> of a piece of writing is the <u>reason</u> why it is written.

➤ Think carefully about the purpose of a text before you begin writing.

➤ Match your <u>vocabulary</u>, <u>style</u> and <u>presentation</u> to the purpose.

A Writing to persuade

KEY FACT

When you write to persuade, you are trying to get your readers to do something.

Writing to persuade includes the following features:

- direct appeal to the reader using questions or the pronoun 'you'

- language used emotively to appeal to the feelings of readers

- punctuation designed to get the reader's attention (e.g. exclamation marks).

The Albert Dock
Liverpool

Exciting shopping!

For shopping that's different, there is nowhere quite like the Albert Dock.

■ Undercover malls house scores of small, individual shops and brightly coloured coster carts displaying an amazing range of merchandise.

■ From toys to treasures, candy to clocks, books to baseball caps, the Dock's got the lot!

■ Fashion-seekers of all ages are well-provided for, with shops selling ladies, men's and children's fashions. Accessories? You'll find no shortage of jewellery, scarves, bags and fragrances to go with that new designer outfit.

■ Souvenir hunting? The Dock can hardly be bettered. There's a staggering range of Beatles mementoes along with items commemorating those other local heroes, Liverpool and Everton Football Clubs. And in between there's everything from a picture postcard or guidebook of the Albert Dock to ships' clocks and other reminders of the city's proud maritime past. "Shop at the Dock" – it's all part of the irresistible Albert Dock experience!

Q How many examples of the features of writing to persuade can you find in this text?

B Writing to advise

KEY FACT

When you write to advise, you are persuading someone to do something.

- It is important to get your audience on your side so that they will take your advice.

- You should show that you understand their feelings and reassure them about their difficulties.

Q How has the writer shown she understands the problems of her readers? Find at least three examples.

HAVE YOU JUST STARTED SECONDARY SCHOOL?

Beginning a new term at school can be a very daunting experience. Your new school will probably be much bigger than your old one and you may worry about finding your way around.

Remember you are not on your own – there are lots of people who will help you. You can ask a teacher or an older student to show you the way if you get lost.

Learning lots of new subjects can be confusing too. Some new students find it hard to remember all of their books and equipment in the first few weeks. It is a good idea to pack your bag the night before and to check your diary to make sure that tou have everything you need.

C *Writing to argue*

When you write to argue, you are getting your readers to accept your point of view.

Q How many facts and how many opinions can you find for both 'Yes' and 'No' in the text below?

Remember
Aim to make the reader share your views by using the words 'we' and 'us'.

- When you write to argue, you include **facts** as well as **opinions** to convince your readers.

- Read the text below. Two opposing points of view are presented here. The features of **writing to argue** have been labelled for you.

reader involved directly   facts to support argument

Fireworks: time for a total ban?

YES Let's bring an end to the dangers of fireworks, and impose a total ban on the things once and for all. This newspaper has already highlighted how a new law banning the sale of dangerous fireworks to children is being ignored by some shop owners in Greater Manchester. Even organised displays aren't safe, as was proved last night, when people, including children, were injured at a display in the West Midlands.

Every year in the build-up to Bonfire Night, Postbag publishes letters from people who are sick and tired of hearing fireworks being left off in their area weeks before November 5. Youngsters terrorise old people and those with pets.

Every year people are maimed and even killed by fireworks, despite all the government's efforts to warn of the dangers. Thoughtless idiots will always ignore the warnings, and innocent people will be hurt, unless we ban all fireworks now.

NO Talk of banning all fireworks is an over-reaction. It is true that people are hurt by them, but nothing can be made completely safe these days, not even crossing the road! For many years fireworks and bonfires have brought lots of enjoyment to generations of people in this country. It is one winter's night when everybody gets out and about and has fun. Banning fireworks would put a lot of people out of work, for one thing. And you could hardly ban fireworks without forbidding people to build bonfires. How on earth could such a ban be imposed?

Last night's display was an unfortunate accident, and people were hurt, but it was a one-off. The vast majority of such displays are safe, and there is no earthly reason why they should not continue to be so. Let us not deny children the pleasure that Fireworks Night can bring.

emotive language   rhetorical question   final opinions clearly stated

PRACTICE

1 Write a leaflet based on your town or a place that you have visited. Your **purpose** is to **persuade** readers to visit the place that you have chosen.

2 Write an article for a school magazine in which you either agree or disagree with a ban on fireworks. Your **purpose** is to present a clear **argument** for your ideas.

3 Write three paragraphs for a booklet called 'Settling in at Secondary School'. Your **purpose** is to **advise** Year 7 students.

THE BARE BONES

➤ When writing, it is very important to match your vocabulary, content and sentence structure to the needs of the reader.
➤ Different types of reader need different styles of writing.

KEY FACT

Q Can you find any more examples of places where the writer has matched his style to meet the needs of the audience – in this case, children?

Remember
Use 'you' to address the reader and ask questions to involve the reader.

Q What do you notice about the vocabulary and sentence structure now? What evidence is there to show that this text has been written to match the needs of an older audience?

Think about the needs of your readers (your <u>audience</u>) when you are planning your work.

Look at this piece of writing, which is aimed at children. Notice that the vocabulary and sentence structure are simple so they can easily be read and understood.

bicycle compared with children's toys

Bicycles

vocabulary repeated – only one idea in a sentence

The first bicycle was a <u>sort of hobby-horse</u> on wheels. It had no pedals so you had to push it forward like a scooter. It was impossible to steer.

informal language

You could steer this bicycle by turning the handle-bars. But you still had to push it along with your feet.

use of **You** to involve the reader

This was one of the first bicycles with <u>pedals</u>. <u>Pedalling</u> was very hard work. The <u>pedals</u> went backwards and forwards and drove the back wheel.

• Study the extract below, which was written for a teenage audience.
• Using the information in the article, as well as your own ideas, write a paragraph entitled 'Choosing a friend' for a PSE textbook.

What makes a good friend?

A friend should be...

Funny Lazy Daring Helpful
Hard-working Serious
Intelligent Rebellious Shy

1 What do you look for in a friend? Do you want someone to laugh with or someone to share your troubles? Do you want someone to moan to about problems with teachers or homework? With a partner, make a list of all the things you look for in a friend.

2 What makes a good friend? Look closely at the qualities in this list. Work with a partner to put the qualities into three categories under these headings:
Very important to me
Fairly important
Not important at all.

• Suggest other qualities not included in the list, but which you think are important.

- The extract below is taken from an article written for an adult audience about teenage gambling.

One-armed bandits

opening statement introduces topic of text →

For many teenagers the lure of the fruit machines is irresistible. The combination of noise, lights and cash incentives make them an attractive form of escapism.

marker introduces new point →

However, many experts now see them as increasingly responsible for the growing number of teenage gamblers. 'Fruit machines are a form of hard gambling,' says Dr Emmanuel Moran of the National Council of Gambling. 'They are compulsive and habit forming.'

marker introduces new point →

In fact, a survey, carried out by the National Housing and Town Planing Council, suggested that more than 300,000 British teenagers spend their school dinner money on fruit machines. Over 130,000 are stealing money from their parents to finance their obsession.

- You will see that this text has been annotated to show you something about the structure of the text.

Markers are used in a text to show that a new point is being introduced.

1 Write a short paragraph to explain one of the following to a younger child:
   - how to make a cup of tea
   - why children have to go to school.

2 Write a short article aimed at alerting parents to the dangers of teenage gambling.

   Here are some ideas to help you:
   - It is believed that the problem of teenage gambling is growing . . .
   - Fruit machines are becoming attractive to teenagers because . . .
   - Gambling is habit-forming . . .

THE BARE BONES

➤ In exams, you may be asked to write a letter for a particular <u>purpose</u> (e.g. to complain, to persuade, to express an opinion).

➤ You may be asked to write for a particular <u>audience</u>. You may be asked to reply to another letter writer or to express your views to a wider audience in a letter to a newspaper.

A Writing for a purpose

Look at the following letters taken from a newspaper and a magazine. Each letter has been written for a different purpose.

> Some letters are written in an <u>informal style</u>, according to the audience and the purpose. For example, a letter to a friend would be written in an informal style.

KEY FACT

Q Can you find an example of vocabulary used informally? Can you find examples of shortened words that help to create an informal style in this letter?

This letter to a magazine has been written in an informal style to express an opinion. Some features of such a letter have been identified for you. Study them carefully.

first paragraph identifies the issue →

expresses opinion →

develops opinion →

Dear BBC Vegetarian Good Food

My girlfriend is a vegetarian and she buys your magazine. I'm not a veggie, but I've noticed you carry advertisements for vegetarian dog food in your publication.

I think it's cruel to force your own preferences on a poor animal that can't choose for itself. I own a dog and I only have to watch him eat to see how much he loves meat. I can't believe he'd be half as fit and healthy without it.

KEY FACT

> A letter on a more serious topic is usually presented in a more <u>formal style</u>.

This letter has been written to **persuade** the reader to adopt the same opinion as the writer. The distinguishing features of this letter have been labelled for you.

first paragraph identifies the issue ←

direct appeal to the reader – use of '**we**' and '**your**' ←

Q Can you find examples of more formal vocabulary and sentence structure in this letter?

emotive language ←

Quiet, please

A year ago the Royal British Legion wrote asking for your readers' support for a two-minute silence at 11am on November 11. Over the past two years, the nation has demonstrated its strong sympathy with the idea.

So <u>we write to seek your support again</u> – for a two-minute silence on Tuesday November 11. The legion hopes that everyone in the country will have, or be offered, the opportunity to pause for two minutes silent reflection at 11am.

We look particularly to parents and teachers to respond to our call again this year. Our children have not known the <u>horror</u> of war, save perhaps through news pictures from Bosnia, the Gulf or elsewhere. We should ensure that they understand the <u>value of peace</u> and security by explaining to them the meaning of remembrance. This year, the Spice Girls have agreed to help.

Graham Downing,
National Chairman,
Royal British Legion, London

B   Making a plan

Always make a plan before you tackle letter-writing in an exam. Think about:

- who will read your letter

- how you will begin your letter

- how many points you will include, four or five is usually sufficient

- number your points in the order in which you will use them

- the sort of ending you will need for your letter; for example, an informal letter to a friend would end with see you soon, a more formal letter would end with yours sincerely

- will you begin with your most powerful point or will you end with it?

Remember
- Always plan before you write.
- Decide whether a formal or an informal tone is needed.

- I am in favour of six school terms per year.

- Improved exam results.

- School work is tiring.

- Teachers would appreciate this change.

- Summer holidays too long – boredom results.

- Strongly disagree with the writer of last week's Letter of the Week.

- Frequent rests useful.

Q Look at this plan made by a student in an exam. Put the points in the right order.

PRACTICE

Write your own letter to a newspaper expressing your views on the introduction of six shorter terms in the school year instead of three long ones as at present.

Your purpose is to express your views clearly and sensibly and to **persuade** readers to agree with you.

THE BARE BONES

➤ Advice sheets are written with a specific purpose in mind: to give advice on a particular topic.

➤ The language and presentation of an advice leaflet is adapted to suit the audience and the topic.

A Looking at language

Q How many imperatives can you find in this text? Find one other way the writer has used to present advice.

1 Some advice sheets use a series of instructions to give advice.

Look at this example:

GETTING INTO GOOD HABITS

● Aim to use less of everything. Stick to instructions and hold back on that extra squirt.

● Ask yourself whether the sink really needs another clean or whether clothes can be aired rather than washed.

● Cleaning products work better in soft water, so you can use less. If you live in a hard-water area, use a softener.

● Do you really need individual cleaners for the different parts of your home?

● Stop buying aerosols, even if they don't contain CFCs.

2 Sometimes advice leaflets use facts to advise readers.

Look at this example:

Q What hidden advice is given to parents in this text?

Most parents, quite rightly, worry about their children trying drugs. They want to know the risks and what to do if they suspect their child is using drugs. But – as many teachers, hospital staff and police officers will tell you – alcohol can cause just as many problems for young people. One thousand children under the age of 15 are admitted to hospital each year with acute alcohol poisoning. Around half of pedestrians aged between 16 and 60 killed in road accidents have more alcohol in their blood than the legal drink drive limit. In 1994, 57,800 people were found guilty or cautioned for drunkenness. The peak age of offenders was 18.

3 Sometimes writers adopt a friendly tone to get readers on their side and to encourage them to take the advice.

Q What features of this writing help the readers to feel that the writer is friendly towards them?

Text messages or phone calls bullying in the 21st century

If you repeatedly receive unpleasant or threatening messages keep a record and tell an adult – even if you know who it is. If it is bullying, it needs dealing with. Remember that seeming upset will show your aggressors that they are winning. Walk tall and be confident. Ignore nasty comments and insults.

B Looking at presentation

- Using pictures and illustrations can make advice leaflets look more interesting and ensure that people will read them closely and take notice of the message.

- Breaking advice down into small chunks marked by bullet points is often used.

- Using colour for different parts can make the advice easier to read.

- Using bold headings and different fonts can emphasise different sections.

Q Can you find examples of all of the presentational devices mentioned above?

Keep safe

On the street
- Keep to main, well-lit pavements.
- Hide mobile phones and valuables from view.
- Keep keys in a pocket rather than a bag.
- Carry a personal alarm. If a car stops and you are threatened, set it off and get away as quickly as possible.
- Walk facing the traffic.
- Carry coins for a phone call.

On buses and trains
- Late at night, sit downstairs near the driver.
- Don't sit close to a lone passenger.
- Don't indicate to others where you will be getting off.

In taxis
- Make sure you use a legal taxi company.
- Avoid mini-cabs or private-hire cars that tout for business.
- Sit behind the driver.

C Writing advice sheets: a summary

1 Choose your language carefully to match that of your readers.

2 When writing for young people, a friendly tone is often the best.

3 Remember, advice sheets can contain facts.

4 Use presentational devices to draw attention to your message.

PRACTICE

Write an advice sheet for school students on how to deal with bullying. Remember to:
- adopt a friendly tone, show that you understand the problem
- give them a range of ways of dealing with bullying
- use presentational devices such as illustrations and different fonts to emphasise your message and to make your advice sheet look interesting.

Writing reports

THE BARE BONES

> Reports usually appear in <u>newspapers</u>. They tell readers about recent events that have happened locally, nationally or internationally. They are written mainly in the <u>past tense</u>.

> Reports can also be written about issues of <u>general concern</u>. They can use a particular event to draw attention to issues. Reports like these are written mainly in the <u>present tense</u>.

A Reporting news

KEY FACT

In a report, the reader's attention is grabbed by the <u>headline</u>. It gives the reader an idea about what will be in the report.

KEY FACT

The first paragraph contains the story's main points. The following paragraphs continue the story and usually give answers to the questions: <u>who, what, where, when, why, how?</u>

Reports include:

- an account of events in the order in which they happened

- a reference to what people have said

- a brief description of people involved in the story

- past-tense verbs, because they refer to events that have already taken place.

Study the report below. Features of report-writing have been labelled for you.

clear headline →

main point of story in first paragraph

brief description

Kaylee sets the pace for a heartfelt celebration

KAYLEE Davidson will be celebrating a very special event on Tuesday – the 10th anniversary of her donor heart.

The lively youngster from Washington, Tyne and Wear who loves to dance, run and play was just five months old when she became the youngest child in Britain to have a successful heart transplant. Yesterday Kaylee was guest of honour at a party in Newcastle for her and 50 other heart transplant children, alive thanks to donor families and surgeons at the city's Freeman Hospital.

Her mother Carol, 29, now vice-chairman of support group Heart Transplant Families Together, said: 'I can't believe 10 years have gone by. Kaylee is a normal little girl and she lives life to the full.'

use of direct speech

B Reporting issues

Reports about issues often give information about a recent happening. Their main focus is to make readers aware of a particular issue.

Read this example closely:

Hitting out

Should parents be allowed to smack their children? Emily Moore looks at the issues.

A 12-year-old boy won the right to go to the European Court of Human Rights in Strasbourg last week because his stepfather beat him with a garden cane when he was nine years old. The hearing may take two years – if the boy wins, smacking could be banned in Britain.

Does British law allow grown-ups to hit children?
Yes it does. Parents have the right to use what is called "reasonable chastisement" to keep their children under control (1933 Children and Young Person's Act). So, parents may hit them, but not hard enough to cause serious injury.

However in 1991, the British government did agree to abide by Article 19 of the United Nation's Convention of the Rights of the Child, which says children should be protected from all forms of physical or mental violence. The UN is "deeply worried" about British law which allows adults to hit children.

Do any countries ban smacking?
Physical punishment of children is illegal in Austria, Cyprus, Denmark, Finland, Norway and Sweden. Sweden banned it in 1979 and studies show that violence against children has declined in the 17 years since then.

Why do parents smack their children?
Most parents were smacked when they were children and some believe it is the best way to stop a child's bad behaviour. All children need to learn the difference between right and wrong – the question is, does smacking teach this?

1 What event is the starting-point for this report?

2 What issue is raised in this report?

3 Where does the report use facts and figures to help the reader understand the issues?

4 How does the report draw the reader's attention to different aspects of the issue?

Q How many features does this report have in common with the previous one?

PRACTICE

1 Using the information in the report above, write your own report on the topic of smacking children.
- Before you begin, make a list of the points that you will include (you can use some of the information from the report above).
- Start with the same information about the twelve-year-old boy.
- Use subheadings to summarise the content of each paragraph.
- Include comments from parents and children, if you wish.

2 Write your own news report based on one of the following:
- the decision by a local council to sell playing fields to make way for a motorway
- gales and torrential rain that have caused damage to houses and flooding.

Use the features labelled opposite in your report.

THE BARE BONES

> Articles cover a wide range of topics depending on the <u>audience</u> and the <u>purpose</u> of the publication in which they appear.

> Some articles are written to give <u>advice.</u> Others are written to <u>inform</u> the reader.

> Articles are written to <u>develop an argument</u> or to <u>present a particular point of view.</u>

A Audience and purpose

Q Where might this article appear? What is its purpose? Who is the audience likely to be? What is the tone? How can you tell?

Articles adopt a <u>different tone</u> and use <u>different vocabulary</u> according to their audience and purpose.

Look at this extract from an article:

> **W**heels are a wonder of the world. Take a look at what they consist of: 32 thin steel wires; 32 brass nipples; a light alloy hoop; and at the centre of the whole thing, a hub. None of the component parts are very strong and all (with the possible exception of the hub), are bendable.
>
> However, give these components to a good wheel builder and within an hour or two they can transform them into lightweight structures capable of supporting upwards of one hundred times their own weight.

B Tone of writing

Articles can be written in an <u>informal tone</u>.

Read this extract from an article written to entertain readers:

Q Can you spot examples of:
- informal language
- use of humour and exaggeration
- places where the writer talks <u>directly</u> to the reader?

Hi-tech, low life

Do computers turn children into spotty, uncommunicative youths? Not always says **Bill O'Neill**

Your seven-year-old daughter is determined to prove that she's now big enough to be a nerd, too. She slips into the back room while the rest of the family is watching Blind Date, switches on the computer and keys in the password (cleverly stuck on the back of the machine so children won't find it).

You're not worried about her coming across an unsolicited invitation among your family e-mail to surf the Internet in search of a "hot new product, try me out", the sort of appeal that thinly disguises a new pornography site; you cancelled your subscription to the company that provided your connection to the Internet more than a month ago because the service was too expensive and getting on-line too unpredictable.

No, your real concern these days is the amount of time that the children spend in front of that damn machine; they seem to be at it all day in school, and then want to do the same in the evenings and at the weekends at home. It'll ruin their eyesight, make them even more uncommunicative than they already are and generally turn them into fat, spotty youths, fit only to be wrapped in an anorak.

Bill O'Neill is editor of on-line. The British and Technology is the third annual report from Motorola: for copies, contact Steve Wyre on 0172 279 0131, or by e-mail on TMKT46@email.mot.com

This article appeals directly to the reader. It uses an **informal** tone, as if the writer is talking directly to the reader.

C Structuring an argument

EY FACT

It is important to <u>structure</u> your argument carefully when <u>presenting your point of view</u> in an argument.

Read this article, which is annotated to show how the argument has been structured.

opening paragraph reveals topic of argument

Gee Mom, TV has made me American

By Sean Poulter Media Correspondent

Children are watching so many American television programmes they are losing touch with British life, a watchdog warned yesterday.

first example used to illustrate argument

Some have such a constant diet of Stateside shows that they believe 911 – the US emergency number – rather than 999 is the one to call in a crisis.

As well as alienating youngsters from their own culture, American TV does not instil the social values British programmes do, said Jocelyn Hay, from the voluntary watchdog Voice of the Listener and Viewer.

marker used to introduce new point

Home-grown shows are more likely to get children thinking about and acting on social issues, she told the group's conference in London. 'With American TV, what we are also losing is the social and educational values linked with British television, such as the children showing compassion and interest in other parts of the world,' she added. 'For instance, when they see something on Rwanda, they go back to school and have a jumble sale.'

argument developed in this paragraph

An invasion of cartoon characters is also squeezing out high-quality children's drama and educational programmes.

word used to introduce new point

Since 1981, cartoons on BBC and ITV have jumped from 10 per cent to around 33 per cent of programming. Yesterday, broadcasters were warned that the 'dumbing down' of children's programmes would eventually filter into general schedules.

strong argument used in final sentence

ITV's Michael Forte said parents should take a bigger role in directing children's viewing.

D Writing hints

When you present your opinions in an article, you should:

- make a list of the points you want to include

- reveal the subject of your article in the opening paragraph

- link ideas and introduce new points with markers (e.g. also, as well as, in addition)

- save a powerful point for the last paragraph.

PRACTICE

1 Write the first paragraph of an article about homework. Your purpose is to entertain readers as well as expressing your own point of view about homework.

Remember to • use **humour** and **exaggeration** • address your reader directly using the pronoun **you** or a question.

2 The article above claims that children are being given too many 'easy' and unchallenging programmes to watch on television. Write your own article in which you put forward your point of view on the type of TV programmes available for children *or* teenagers.

Exam questions and model answers

Literary texts

Questions on Simon Armitage

> 1 What do you learn about the speaker of the poem in 'It ain't what you do it's what it does to you' and the speaker of another poem by Simon Armitage?

Preparing your answer

- Look for the key words in the question: 'learn' and 'speaker'. Concentrate your response on the speaker of each poem and what you have learned about him.

- Choose your other poem carefully. Make sure the speaker of your chosen poem makes an interesting comparison. For this question, a good choice would be the speaker of 'I am very bothered'.

- Make a quick plan of the main points you want to make and the quotations you will use to support your points.

Model answer

Opens with clear, straightforward statement

Quotations in brackets keep argument flowing

Quotations integrated into sentence

Wherever possible, draw conclusions from your observations.

Remember that language indicates meaning.

Another key conclusion drawn from the evidence.

The speaker in the poem 'It ain't what you do it's what it does to you' has lived an ordinary life 'in Manchester'. He has done ordinary things ('skimmed flat stones') in ordinary places ('Black Moss'). He compares his humdrum existence with more exotic possibilities: bumming across America or visiting the Taj Mahal in India.

But he finds similarities in the different types of experiences. There was uncertainty and danger in the American experience. He was running out of money ('a dollar to spare') and he carried a knife. In England he lived a dangerous existence 'among thieves'.

He suggests which experience he prefers. When he is describing the Taj Mahal, he says he has not 'padded' through that building, 'listening to the space between/each footfall'. The words 'padded' and the 'space between' make the Taj Mahal sound remote. When it comes to skimming stones on Black Moss, he could 'hear' each set of ripples and 'feel' the stone's inertia. This shows he is a practical sort of person who prefers reality to the world of the imagination.

He shows his real preference in the final stanzas. He compares what it would be like to make a parachute jump to his actual experience of helping out in a day centre. When making the drop, he is playing with experience ('toyed with a parachute cord'), but in the day centre he 'held' the boy's head and 'stroked' his hands. Clearly he is the type of person who prefers everyday experience to some kind of romantic ideal.

He finds it difficult to explain the effect of this experience. He talks about a 'sense of something else'. He concludes by referring to 'that feeling'. He cannot define it. He simply says 'I mean'.

Leave this point unfinished – you will return to it later.

Clear opening statement	The speaker in 'I am very bothered' seems to be a sadistic person, who loves playing practical jokes. He describes a trick played on a girl in the chemistry lab at school, holding out the handle of a pair of red-hot scissors for a girl to take. He seems to delight in causing pain: 'O the unrivalled stench.' He even makes light of the joke: 'then called your name'.
Development of point	
Valid example given to support point	
	But there are other sides to the speaker. At the end of the poem, he suggests the trick might have been his way of asking her to marry him: 'Don't believe me, please, if I say . . .' He might have caused her pain to hide his embarrassment: 'just my butter-fingered way'.
Development linked to the preceding paragraph	
	On the other hand, he might be the sort of person who finds love cruel: 'couldn't shake off the two burning rings.' Whichever type of person he is, he ends by stating: 'I am very bothered.'
Always be aware of different possibilities.	
Personal response based on the argument so far	So, I find both speakers puzzling. Although the speaker of the first poem does state which type of experience he prefers, he cannot really define what he feels about it. The speaker in the second poem does not actually say what he feels about the practical joke. He ends by stating he is 'very bothered', but throughout the poem he seems to be hiding his real feelings. The first speaker seems to be searching for the meaning of his experiences, whilst the second speaker appears to be hiding his true feelings.

Conclusion that answers the question

---

2 Show how Simon Armitage uses structure to help the reader to understand 'Cataract operation' and one other poem.

Preparing your answer

- Remember to look for the key words in the question: 'how', 'structure' and 'helps . . . to understand'.

- Analyse the structure to show how it helps your understanding.

- Choose your second poem carefully.

Here are some ideas on 'Cataract operation' to get you started:

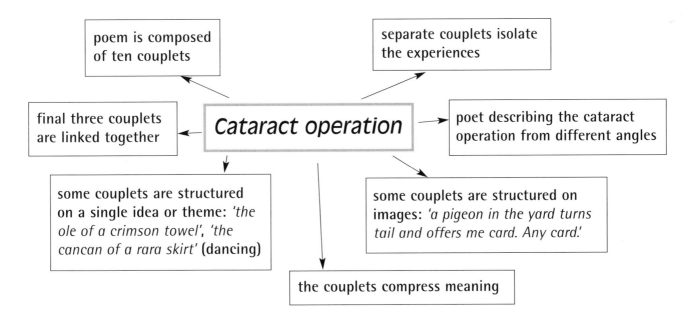

poem is composed of ten couplets

separate couplets isolate the experiences

final three couplets are linked together

Cataract operation

poet describing the cataract operation from different angles

some couplets are structured on a single idea or theme: *'the ole of a crimson towel'*, *'the cancan of a rara skirt'* (dancing)

the couplets compress meaning

some couplets are structured on images: *'a pigeon in the yard turns tail and offers me card. Any card.'*

Carol Ann Duffy

1 In 'In Mrs Tilscher's class' and in one other poem of your choice, show how Duffy uses language to explore a place.

Preparing your answer

- Look for the key words and phrases: 'how', 'language' 'to explore a place'.

- Choose your other poem carefully.

- Make sure the language of your chosen poem makes an interesting comparison. For this question, a good choice would be 'War photographer'.

Model answer

Straightforward opening sentence

Development of first point

Links with preceding paragraph

Quotations used as part of the argument

Change of direction

Look for what is implied by the language.

How atmosphere is created

Use quotations to develop the argument.

Nature is used by writers to suggest what people are feeling.

In the opening stanza, Duffy uses words associated with school to create the classroom atmosphere: 'chalky', 'opened with a long pole'. The language suggests a school room of long ago ('Mrs Tilscher chanted the scenery'), when learning was done through repetition. The world of education that Duffy recreates is a happy one, as shown in the 'laugh of a bell'.

This feeling of happiness is continued into the second stanza. The classroom was even 'better than home' and the books were 'enthralling'. But the mood changes with the mention of the moors murderers Brady and Hindley. Nevertheless, the young Duffy feels protected. She says that the memory lasted as long as a 'smudge of a mistake' in her written work. The happy atmosphere is continued in the reward of a gold star and the pleasure taken in shaving a pencil slowly.

A dramatic change occurs in the next stanza. It begins with the tadpoles changing into frogs. Their development is seen in terms of a language lesson ('changed/from commas into exclamations'). The exclamation marks sound a warning. A boy tells the young Duffy about the facts of life. The point about him being 'rough' suggests the news is unpleasant.

Her growing sexual awareness is continued in the final stanza. The poet creates an atmosphere of excitement ('the air tasted of electricity'). The young Duffy could feel the change ('tangible'). Even the weather changed. The sky was heavy, 'sexy' even. It seemed to press in upon her. She was anxious to know 'how you were born'. She felt different from the girl in the first stanza. Now she was 'impatient' to grow up away from the school. The thunderstorm marks a change in her life. Her innocent days have been destroyed ('split open').

In 'War photographer', Duffy uses language to present different worlds. At home, the photographer is seen to be engaged in a sacred type of work. Duffy compares him to a priest 'intoning a mass'. He is engaged in developing his films 'Of suffering'. But he feels relatively calm: 'the pain is ordinary'. The 'simple' weather emphasises this feeling of calm, though his hands 'seem to' tremble.

Draws two strands together	The world of the battlefield is conveyed in horrific terms: 'blood stained into foreign dust'. He captures the terror in his photographs: 'A hundred agonies in black and white'. He joins these separate worlds together in his darkroom. The developing picture gradually takes shape as 'a half-formed ghost' – an image to come back to haunt him.
Development of first point.	A third world is the one of newspaper readers. They seem to be affected by the photographs ('The reader's eyeballs prick/with tears') but the sympathy is short-lived. It only lasts between the 'bath and pre-lunch beers'.
Moves from one world into another	In these poems, language is used to create worlds of different experiences. In 'Mrs Tilscher's class', Duffy traces her early development from innocence to sexual awakening. She comes to see life from a different perspective, where even the sky is 'sexy'. In 'War photographer', Duffy contrasts the relative feelings of calm at home with the sufferings on the battlefield.
Different worlds linked together.	She links the two places through the images developing in the photographer's tray.

> **2** Show how in 'Stealing', and one other poem, Duffy uses language to reveal the speaker of the poem.

Preparing your answer

Look for the key words and phrases: 'language', 'reveal the speaker'.
Choose your second poem carefully: 'Valentine' would be a good choice here.
Find examples of different ways in which language is used.
Here are some ideas on 'Stealing' to get you started:

- starts in mid-conversation: *The most unusual thing I ever stole?*
- use of single-word sentences for dramatic effect: *Midnight. Again. Again*
- use of single-word sentences to make the reader read between the lines: *Mirrors*
- justifies what he is doing: *Better off dead than giving in*
- confesses to the reader: *sometimes I steal things*

Ted Hughes

> 1 How does Ted Hughes present the power of nature in 'The wind' and in another poem of your choice.

Preparing your answer

- Look for the **key words**: 'how', 'power of nature'. Concentrate your response on the **methods** that Ted Hughes adopts.

- Make sure the **language** of your chosen poem makes an interesting comparison. For this question, a good choice would be 'Hawk roosting'.

Model answer

Straightforward comment	The poet uses alliteration and assonance to emphasise the violence and cruelty of nature: 'Through the brute wind that dented the balls of my eyes'. The hammering sound of the 'b' sound emphasises the wind's power. The 'oo' sound of 'Through' and 'brunt' catch the eerie noise made by the wind. In this way, Hughes establishes both the noise and the power of the wind.
Immediate supporting quotation	
Explains the effect of language use	This wind's strength is further increased by the poet's use of rhythm: 'Black gull bent like an iron bar slowly'. By putting the rhythmical stress on the monosyllables 'Black', 'gull', 'bent' and 'bar', Ted Hughes presents a picture in sound of heavy gusts of wind. The use of monosyllables makes them into hammer blows beating on the house. He cleverly changes the speed at the end of the line with 'slowly'. This makes the reader experience the strain of the gull being bent gradually. This feeling of tension is sustained in 'strained its guyrope'.
Develops the argument of first paragraph	
Includes the effect on the reader	
Shows different types of violence	The metaphors and similes express a violent world: 'flung a magpie away'. The poet sees madness in the wind: 'Flexing like the lens of a mad eye'. He compares the wind to animals out of control: 'stampeding the fields'. The wind is pictured as a swordsman attacking mankind: 'wind wielded/blade-light'. The poet imagines the wind invading the world of man: 'feel the roots of the house move'. It is as if nature herself is uprooting man's civilisation.
Draws out the significance of the argument	
Gets to the key effect of the violent language	The violence is summed up in how the people react to it. The people try to hide 'deep/In chairs'. They are clearly frightened: 'we grip/Our hearts'. Ted Hughes increases their terror by imagining the stones themselves being terrified: 'the stones cry out'. With this subtle use of personification, Hughes reveals the extent of the horror.
Links to previous poem and makes a separate point	The power of nature is present in 'Hawk roosting', but less obviously. Hughes finds the power of nature in the bird. The hawk is seen as a powerful king controlling his subjects: 'I kill where I please'. Nature, like one of his subjects, supports him. She provides him with cover: 'The convenience of the high trees'. She physically supports him when he is flying: 'The air's buoyancy'. The hawk's power is not expressed through alliteration and assonance, but is felt in the hawk's absolute control.
Shows a significant difference	

Shows clearly where the power lies	Similarly, nature is felt to be powerful, but not through violent language. Quietly, Hughes states that 'It took the whole of Creation' to produce the bird. The power is contained in the length of time it took to make such a creature. Then the poet turns the argument upside down. The bird actually controls nature: 'Now I hold creation in my foot.' The hawk states that nature is on his side: 'The sun is behind me.' On the surface, this means that the sun is shining behind him. But it could mean that the sun supports the bird ('I'm right behind you').
Looks for meaning in ambiguities	
Always emphasise the climax of a poem.	Finally, the poet shows the hawk's absolute control. The bird comments that nothing has changed 'since I began'. He is going to keep it that way: 'I am going to keep things like this.'
Summarises the language use in both poems	So, Ted Hughes expresses the power of nature in both these poems. In the first, he uses stylistic devices (alliteration, assonance, rhythm, etc.) to dramatic effect. In the second, his more subtle approach manages to convey the control that nature has through the dominance of the bird.

---

2 How does Hughes use language to present different worlds in 'The warm and the cold' and one other poem?

Preparing your answer

- Look for the key words: 'how', 'language' and ' different worlds'.

- Choose your second poem carefully. 'Work and play' would be an appropriate choice.

- Find examples of language use and explain their effect.

Here are some ideas to get you started:

- Violent similes to convey the world of a winter night: *Like a slow trap of steel*

- The outside world seems to be mad: *Has lost her wits*

- The outside world is seen to be very old: *Like a mammoth of ice*

- Use of contrast in the similes to create a world of hibernating creatures:

    But the carp is in its depth

    Like a planet in its heaven

- Use of domestic comfort in the similes:

    And the badger in its bedding

    Like a loaf in the oven

- Use of puzzling similes:

    The flies are behind the plaster

    Like the lost score of a jig

Poems from other cultures and traditions

1 Explain how two poets from your selection present cultural differences.
  Show how the differences are presented in 'Presents from my aunts in Pakistan'
  by Moniza Alvi and in one other poem of your choice.

Preparing your answer

- Look for the key words: 'how', 'present', 'cultural differences'. In your response, concentrate on the methods used by the two poets.

- Choose your other poem carefully.

- Make sure the method used by the poet of your chosen poem makes an interesting comparison with Moniza Alvi's method. For this question, a good choice would be 'Nothing's changed' by Tatamkhulu Afrika.

Model answer

Clear opening statement	In 'Presents from my aunts in Pakistan', the poet uses clothing as symbols of cultural differences. In the first stanza, she presents a picture of traditional culture. The clothes that her aunts sent are brightly coloured and superficially attractive. One salwar kameez is 'peacock-blue', another 'like an orange split open'.
Relevant examples	
Develops the argument by introducing a contrast	But not all is as attractive as it seems. The 'candy-striped bangles . . . drew blood'. The salwar bottoms were 'broad and stiff'. The fact that the garment felt uncomfortable shows how awkward the poet felt about traditional dress.
Express the significance of symbols	Instead, she preferred a western style of living, as in 'denim and corduroy'. The fact that she 'longed for' shows how strongly she felt about this. On the other hand, she felt her traditional costume 'cling to her'. She felt 'aflame'. This might suggest that she was embarrassed by the old style of dress, which she blushed to be seen in.
Develops the argument through an alternative	Moreover, she felt trapped by the old way of life: 'I couldn't rise up out of its fire.' She felt ashamed of the presents. Though they were bright and attractive, 'radiant', she kept them hidden away 'in my wardrobe'.
Expresses the significance	Other characters are used by the poet to show cultural differences. Her aunts back home, dressed in traditional costume, wanted a change. They 'requested cardigans/from Marks and Spencers'. Her school friend was not impressed by the poet's present.
Useful word to indicate development	
Looks for other expressions of culture	At the end, the reader is presented with a picture of the society where the aunts live. They are pictured 'screened from visitors', living 'in shaded rooms'. The impression given is one of women hidden away from society, a status that the poet now sees as alien to her.
Neat comparative link	The poet of 'Nothing's changed' also presents a picture of cultural alternatives. He presents two contrasting environments. His preferred environment is the one that he has traditionally inhabited. In his natural home, the land has gone to seed, but the weeds are 'amiable'. It is a friendly place.
Expresses the significance	

This paragraph explains the significance of key symbols. →

His area has been designated for development. It has no name, known impersonally as 'District Six'. The new buildings have a raw feeling: 'brash', 'flaring'. They appear ugly and 'squat'. There is a feeling that the poet and his people will be excluded: 'guard at the gatepost'. He uses the symbol of glass to present his predicament. He can see through the glass, but it presents a barrier: 'I press my nose'.

He expresses his anger. He wants a stone or bomb 'to shiver down the glass'. But he is left helpless. Nothing will happen. 'Nothing's changed'.

Brief summary shows similarity and differences →

So, although the poets express cultural differences in different ways, one through clothing and the other through a changed environment, they both feel trapped between two worlds.

---

2 How is the influence of one culture on another shown in 'Half-caste' and one other poem?

Preparing your answer

- Look for the key words: 'how', 'influence', 'culture'.

- Choose your second poem carefully. 'Ogun' or 'Charlotte O'Neil's song' would be appropriate choices.

- Start with the fact that a 'half-caste' is a product of two cultures. Search for examples of what the poet has to say about different cultures.

Here are some ideas to get you started:

- Poet as a half-caste sees the world as half of one thing and half of another:
  half-caste weather, I close half an eye

- He writes in two languages: standard English and West Indian Patois:
  Excuse me/wha yu mean

- He uses symbols of western culture: Picasso and Tchaikovsky

- He sees two cultures in these symbols:
  Black key wid a white key

- Jokes about his cultural position:
  cast half a shadow.

Non-fiction texts

Reading

How does this text inform, persuade and advise the reader?

Comment on:

- what the advertisement contains
- how the material is presented
- the language it uses.

One of these tomatoes is contaminated by E.coli

(If you can't tell which, don't worry.)

Food poisoning is on the increase.

E.coli bacteria have now been found not just on meat, but on the surface of fruit and vegetables too. (They'd been fertilised with contaminated manure.)

To make matters worse, certain types of E.coli have even developed a resistance to some antibiotics.

Isn't anything safe to eat any more?

The good news is, E.coli bacteria have a deadly enemy: Milton Fluid.

In fact Milton, when diluted with water and used as recommended, kills all germs.

No wonder more and more people are buying it, whether there's a baby in the house or not.

And they're using it not just on their fridges, kitchen surfaces and chopping boards, but also for rinsing fruit and salad vegetables.

Perhaps doing that sounds a bit odd, eccentric even.

If it does, why not try this test for yourself: following the instructions on the pack, rinse some tomatoes, grapes or other fruit in diluted Milton, then let them drain until the surface is completely dry.

When you come to eat them, you'll find that Milton hasn't even changed the taste at all. (Even though it will have killed germs by the million.)

Better still, fruit and veg rinsed in Milton stay fresh for days longer.

That's because Milton kills the bacteria that make food go off, as well as the ones that cause food poisoning.

Maybe it's not such an odd thing to do after all. More like common sense, in fact.

Especially when the alternative is just hoping for the best.

FAMILY PROTECTION FROM FOOD GERMS

Answering this type of question

A What skills do I need?

You are expected to:

1 write about the content of the text, showing that you understand the writer's argument

2 comment on presentational devices such as headlines, illustrations, different types of font

3 give examples of the writer's language and show how this matches the purpose of the text

4 explain how readers will react to the text.

B Extra tips

To do well when answering questions on reading non-fiction, you should follow these steps:

1 Read the question first and then skim-read the text.

2 Underline the key words in the question and then scan the text for details that you will need to answer the question.

3 Remember to refer closely to the text, using either quotations or your own words.

4 Always include references to the purpose and audience of a text.

C Remember:

1 to follow the bullet-points closely – they are your guide to writing exactly what the examiner expects

2 this question carries the highest number of marks, so make sure you answer in detail.

Model answer

Includes reference to key word in question

Comments on language in early part of answer

Quotation used to support point

Able to analyse the effect of presentational devices

Pays attention to the details of the text

Shows understanding of layout in the advertisement

The first paragraph contains information about food-poisoning bacteria. The scientific name is used, which convinces readers that this is a serious article. The main part of the article tells readers about how Milton fluid can be used to destroy bacteria. The writers have used this information to give readers advice about safe food preparation. The article persuades readers to buy Milton fluid by convincing them that it kills all germs. It uses the phrase 'common sense', which makes the reader think that using Milton Fluid is a very good idea.

The presentation is eye-catching. The bold headline 'One of these tomatoes is contaminated by E.coli' is an effective way to catch the reader's attention because 'contaminated' is such a dramatic word. This caption is written in an uneven font, which also catches the reader's eye.

The small caption at the bottom of the advertisement – 'family protection from food germs' – is a reminder of the advertisement's purpose to persuade readers that Milton Fluid is safe and therefore that they should buy it.

There is a lot of writing in the advert, which might put some readers off, but the paragraphs are short, which will make reading easier and so encourage readers to take in the message. The advertisement persuades readers by using an informal tone; it sounds as if someone is talking directly to them. For example, 'If you can't tell which, don't worry.' The use of the word 'you' appeals directly to the reader, as does the use of the question, 'Isn't anything safe to eat any more?'

Able to summarise argument

Addresses focus of question

Shows clear awareness of purpose of text

Analyses language and its effect on the reader.

Non-fiction

Writing

Use this information about bullying to write an advice sheet for parents.

The Balance of Playground Power

- One in five children in Britain is either a bully or a victim of bullying. Some researchers believe this is just the tip of the iceberg: they think more like 70 per cent of the school population is involved.

- A pilot study of 4,000 primary schoolchildren for Kidscape, the children's safety group, revealed that 38 per cent had been bullied, and that bullying was one of children's main worries.

- Male bullies outnumber female bullies three to one. Boys bully both sexes, girls generally tend to stick to their own sex.

- There is a higher incidence of bullying in urban schools than in rural schools.

- Statistics say 68 per cent of all school bullies will become violent adults. A bully has a 25 per cent chance of committing crime in adult life (the average is five per cent).

- Strong links have been established between truancy, underacheivement and bullying.

Answering this type of question

A What skills do I need?

You are expected to:

1 match the style of your writing to your audience and purpose, in this case the **audience** is **adults** and the **purpose** is to **advise**

2 organise your ideas so that your readers can easily follow your ideas

3 use some presentational devices to attract and hold the attention of your audience.

B Extra tips

To do well in writing non-fiction texts in examination conditions, you should follow these steps:

1 plan your work before you write

2 choose your words carefully and aim to use a wide range of vocabulary.

C Remember:

1 to check your work for mistakes as you are writing – check after every paragraph, as it is easier to correct mistakes at this stage

2 to read through your work when it is finished, to check for spelling and punctuation mistakes.

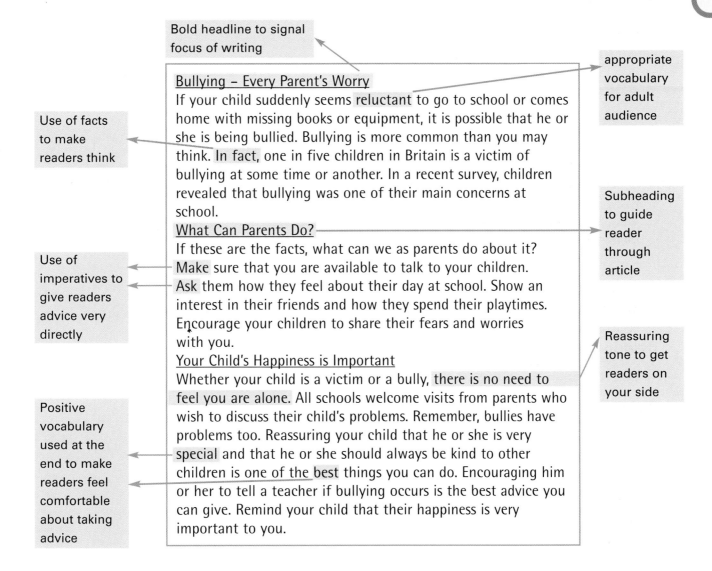

Bold headline to signal focus of writing

appropriate vocabulary for adult audience

Use of facts to make readers think

Use of imperatives to give readers advice very directly

Subheading to guide reader through article

Reassuring tone to get readers on your side

Positive vocabulary used at the end to make readers feel comfortable about taking advice

Bullying – Every Parent's Worry

If your child suddenly seems reluctant to go to school or comes home with missing books or equipment, it is possible that he or she is being bullied. Bullying is more common than you may think. In fact, one in five children in Britain is a victim of bullying at some time or another. In a recent survey, children revealed that bullying was one of their main concerns at school.

What Can Parents Do?

If these are the facts, what can we as parents do about it? Make sure that you are available to talk to your children. Ask them how they feel about their day at school. Show an interest in their friends and how they spend their playtimes. Encourage your children to share their fears and worries with you.

Your Child's Happiness is Important

Whether your child is a victim or a bully, there is no need to feel you are alone. All schools welcome visits from parents who wish to discuss their child's problems. Remember, bullies have problems too. Reassuring your child that he or she is very special and that he or she should always be kind to other children is one of the best things you can do. Encouraging him or her to tell a teacher if bullying occurs is the best advice you can give. Remind your child that their happiness is very important to you.

Other writing questions you will find in examinations

- You could also be asked to write to persuade.

For example:

Write a letter to your headteacher persuading him or her to improve facilities for Year 11 students in your school.

- Or you could be asked to write to argue.

For example:

Write an article for a magazine read by parents in which you argue the case for the abolition of homework.

Literary texts

Simon Armitage

Cataract operation   Complete this chart:

Word/phrase	Suggested ideas
Turtleneck	
Offers me a card	
Monkey business	
Cheerio of a handkerchief	
Struts	

About his person   Complete this chart:

Objects found on the person	Suggests about that person
Library card	
Postcard	
Diary	
Analogue watch	
Shopping list	

I am very bothered

Complete the following statements:

- 'the handles in the naked flame' suggests that he is the sort of person who . . .
- 'then called your name' shows how . . .
- 'O the unrivalled stench' makes him sound as if he is . . .
- 'that was just my butterfingered way' is his excuse . . .

It ain't what you do

Fill in the spaces in this paragraph about this poem:

When the poet talks about living in Manchester, he says he has been living with _____ .
He says to bum around America with only a dollar to spare would have been _____ .
Clearly he prefers the _____ experience of skimming stones across Black Moss to
padding through the Taj Mahal, where the phrase _____ suggests he is not actually
walking on the marble floor. When he compares parachute dropping with
helping out in a care centre, the words _____ tell the reader it is real experience. His
bodily reaction to this experience is expressed in the phrase _____ .

Duffy

Before you were mine

Complete this chart:

Phrases from the poem	Tells you what Duffy admires about her mother
Blows round your legs	
You reckon it's worth it	
Small bites on your neck	
Stamping stars from the wrong pavement	

War photographer

Fill in the blanks of this paragraph about a war photographer.

In the first stanza, the poet compares the war photographer to a _____ through the phrase _____ . In the second stanza, he is clearly affected by the work that he has to do, but the phrase _____ shows that the suffering is quite mild. Later in the poem, he describes the suffering on the battlefield to be quite different in such a phrase as _____ . The word _____ suggests he does not seem to care about the suffering below.

Stealing

Complete the following:

Words in context	Suggests about the character of the thief
I wanted him	
Life's tough	
I'm a mucky ghost	
Again. Again.	

In Mrs Tilscher's class

Complete the following:

Phrases from the poem	Tells you what the young Duffy is feeling
Glowed like a sweet shop	
Uneasy smudge of a mistake	
Tangible alarm	
The sky split open	

Ted Hughes

Hawk roosting

Complete this chart:

The behaviour of the hawk	Suggests he is
I sit in the top of the wood	
For my inspection	
Tearing off heads	
My eye has permitted	

The warm and the cold

Complete the following:

Comparison	Suggests the tone
Like a planet in its heaven	
Like a doll in its lace	
Like a key in a purse	
Like money in a pig	

Tractor

Fill in the missing words or phrases from this piece about 'Tractor':

The poem concerns starting a tractor on a winter morning. In the second stanza, the phrase _____ suggests the work is like a battle. In the next stanza, the poet suggests the work is torture through the phrase _____ .The continuous use of alliteration, as in _____ , and assonance, as in _____ , helps create a feeling of _____ . Eventually, the suffering turns to victory. This is celebrated in the word _____ .

Wind

Indicate the rhythm of the following lines, by putting a forward slash over the stressed syllables:

The woods crashing through darkness, the booming hills

Blade-light, luminous black and emerald

And feel the roots of the house move, but sit on

Hearing the stones cry out under the horizons

Poems from other cultures and traditions

from 'Unrelated incidents'   Complete this chart:

Phrase	Suggests about the speaker's attitude to his audience
Thi reason/a talk wia/BBC accent	
Lik wanna yoo/scruff	
This/is ma trooth	
Yi canny talk/right	

Half-caste   Complete the following:

Symbols of half-caste culture	Contains the two halves of . . .
Picasso	
Half-caste weather	
England weather	
Tchaikovsky	

Presents from my aunts in Pakistan

Fill in the gaps from this piece on 'Presents from my aunts in Pakistan' with words or phrases from the poem:

The poet pictures two separate cultures through symbols of clothing. In the first stanza, she uses such descriptions as _____ to create a society of beauty. However, some fashions give a feeling of discomfort, as in _____ , as though the poet feels she does not quite belong in this society. She prefers western clothing, as in her reference to _____ . She feels slightly embarrassed about fashions from her country of origin. She keeps her presents in her _____ .

Nothing's changed   Complete this chart:

Descriptions of place	Suggests the speaker's attitude to that place
Amiable weeds	
Brash with glass	
Haute cuisine	
Spit a little on the floor	

Non-fiction texts
Reading

Extracting information

1 Before you read the text, you should read the question first – True or False?

2 When you skim read a text, you are looking for particular details – True or False?

3 Underlining parts of the text does not really help you to extract information – True or False?

Distinguishing between fact and opinion

1 Complete these statements by filling in the gaps:

Facts are _____ .

2 Facts often contain _____ .

3 Opinions are p_____ ; they are what someone b_____ .

4 Words that often introduce an opinion are: appear _____

_____ .

Following an argument

1 Following an argument means _____ .

2 A good way to work out the writer's _____ is to _____ key _____ .

3 To present their argument, writers often use both _____ and _____ .

Identifying purpose and audience

1 The purpose of a text is (a) the reason a reader reads it or (b) the reason it was written.

2 Sort out the jumbled letters to make purposes for writing:

naxilpe   sedvai   uderseap   tutsrinc   minfro   tentrenai

Understanding presentation

1 The appearance of texts on the page is known as _____ .

2 Headlines can be made to appear eye-catching by _____ .

3 Charts and diagrams are used to _____ .

Evaluating language

1 Imperatives are used to _____ .

2 Emotive language is used to _____ .

3 Writers use questions to _____ .

Comparing texts

This means writing about the _____ and _____ between texts.

Non-fiction texts

Writing

Writing for a specific purpose

1 Three features of writing to persuade are:

a)

b)

c)

2 Colloquial language is

a) formal   b) informal.

3 When you write to argue, you are getting your readers to _____ .

4 When you write to advise, you are _____ .

Matching writing to your audience

1 You need to match these three things to the needs of your reader:

a)

b)

c)

2 Different types of readers need _____ .

Writing letters

1 A letter to a friend would be written in an _____ style.

2 Before you tackle letter-writing in an exam, you should always _____ .

Writing advice sheets

1 Which of the following can be used to give advice:

a) facts   b) rules   c) instructions?

2 You can encourage readers to take your advice by _____ .

Writing reports

1 Reports include:

a)

b)

c)

d)

Writing articles

1 Articles can be written to _____ .

2 They adopt a different _____ and _____ according to their _____ and _____ .

Glossary

This glossary provides a quick and handy reference to some of the terms used in this book. Use it to check you understand the words and that you can use them correctly in your own answers.

Alliteration

repeating consonants that sound the same at the beginning of words or stressed syllables. *Example: Peter Piper picked a peck of pickled peppers.*

Argument

the meaning a writer wants to convey in a piece of writing.

Assonance

giving the impression that words sound similar by repeating the same or similar vowel sounds. *Example: marrows and carrots.*

Brainstorming

writing down all the various possible meanings and interpretations you can think of after reading a particular piece of writing.

Colloquialism

an informal word, phrase or piece of English you might use when chatting. *Example: saying* spud *instead of* potato.

Context

the text which surrounds a word or phrase. A word may fit into its context or may appear to surprise you and be out of context.

Cross-referencing

reading or writing about the different works of an author or authors to point out similarities in content and/or types of expression.

Dialogue

conversation between characters.

Emotive language

words or phrases that arouse an emotional response in the reader. *Example: the poor, defenceless animals.*

Figure of speech

where the meaning of a particular expression isn't the same as the literal meaning of the words. *Example: she was over the moon with joy.*

Foregrounding/highlighting

when the author begins consecutive sentences or lines of verse with the same words or structure.

Imagery/images

is the general term to cover figures of speech (metaphor, simile, etc.). Through the use of imagery a writer projects different images to the reader/listener.

Irony

using language to express the opposite to what you mean or feel.

Metaphor

describing something by saying it is another thing. *Example: he's a wizard at Maths. (c.f. simile)*

Narrative method/style

how the author tells a story in a piece of writing.

Paradox

a statement that appears to contradict itself. *Examples: cold fire, sick health*

Personification

giving things or ideas human characteristics. *Example: the hot fat spat in the pan.*

Prose

a form of writing that is not in verse and that doesn't rhyme. Novels and newspapers are written in prose.

Rhyme

using pairs or groups of words, usually at the end of lines of verse, which have the same or very similar sounds.

Rhyme scheme

used to discuss the way a poem rhymes. Write 'A' to denote the sound of the last word of the first line. If the second line ends with the same sound, write 'A' again. If it's different, write 'B'. Do the same thing with all the lines in the poem. You might find that the rhyme scheme of a poem with three four-line stanzas is AABB, or ABAB, or ABCA, etc.

Rhyming couplet

two consecutive lines of verse that rhyme with each other, and are usually about the same length. If the rhyme scheme of a poem is AABBCC and so on, the poem is written in rhyming couplets.

Rhythm

a term usually applied to poetry, but which can also be used for drama and prose. Rhythm is produced by the stress given to words when they are read aloud. If the stress falls on words at regular intervals, this is called regular rhythm. If the stress falls with no particular pattern, this is called irregular rhythm.

Simile

describing something by saying it is *like* or *as* something else. *Example: I've been working like a dog. (c.f. metaphor)*

Soliloquy

a speech spoken by an actor alone on stage, designed to reveal the character's innermost thoughts and feelings.

Sonnet

a poem containing fourteen lines.

Stanza

a poem is usually divided into lines grouped together called stanzas. In hymn-books they are called verses, but make sure you use the word *stanza* in poetry.

Symbol

a word that stands for an object and what it represents. Many poets use their own personal symbols. Carol Ann Duffy uses 'onion' as her valentine.

Texture

the pattern of rhythm and sound in a poem. A piece of material has a texture built up by the threads used to make it and the way it is woven. Poetry has a texture too, made by the words used and the way they are used.

Verse

a term applied to poetic writing, not prose. Note that a verse (singular) is a single line of a poem.

Word association

using words whose meaning can be used to suggest another meaning. The word *red*, for example, means a colour, but it can also suggest danger or a political belief.

The answers here are for the non-fiction section only, because the questions about literary texts often ask you to write a piece of text using your own ideas or opinions. If you want to check your progress on these questions, you could ask your teacher to look at your answers.

Reading

Non-fiction texts

Practice question

- *Voting leaflet:* information leaflet, anyone over 18 years old
- *Castle:* written to inform, would appear in encyclopaedia, audience adult or child
- *Your health:* written to instruct, audience anyone who cooks, appear in magazine

Extracting and collating information

Check question

Six ways in which the RSPCA helps animals are:
- gives first aid and medication to rescued animals
- builds and runs animal shelters
- gives veterinary care to tortured animals
- has wildlife hospitals for treating animals
- returns wild animals to wild

Practice question

- Dolphins are threatened by: pollution, over-fishing, capture and drowning in fishing nets.
- Rhinos are threatened by hunters who kill them for their horns.

Distinguishing between fact and opinion

Check questions

Examples of emotive language:
- 'sorry picture'
- 'disgraceful one'

For just £1 a week: fact
Isn't that a pound well spent: opinion

Look out for these words:
- 'seem to put car security'
- 'they should be making . . .'
- 'the car-makers must take more action'.

Practice question

Facts:
Alarms set off either the car horn or their own sounder; many alarms also knock out the car's ignition; alarms can be triggered by vibration; many alarms only go off for a limited time; some alarms stopped even though the door was open; many alarms are worked by a flick switch inside; a few systems worked with the car's ignition switch; some alarms are more prone to accidental triggering than others.

Opinions:
Using the car's horn might be a bit of a risk; the thief could open the bonnet; people nearby might take notice; this is obviously a worthwhile protection; the sooner the alarm goes the better; sensible as it avoids too much rumpus; a cut-off could be bad; the alarm's switch is a weak point; simple flick switches are quite convenient.

Following an argument

Check questions

Difficulties:
Social pressure, people were shocked; Mum hates hospitals; her mental state was deteriorating.

Positive results:
The home she will go to looks excellent; she will be well cared for; she will have all her meals cooked for her; she will have people around her; mother and daughter have become closer.

Turning point in argument: 'Now I know . . .'

Practice questions

1 The Queen says it is hard for an older person to keep up with the modern world.
2 Ludovic Kennedy says it's difficult for old people to adapt to the fast pace of change in the modern world.
3 Barbara Cartland says we need to go back to the ways of the past.
4 Tony Benn questions whether or not a monach is needed in the modern world.
5 Betty Felsted is 70 years old and does not have any problems in keeping up with the modern world.
6 Ludovic Kennedy, because he says: 'What she has said is absolutely right.'

Identifying purpose and audience

Check questions

Newspapers are written to inform and sometimes to entertain.

Features from text matching arrows:
- numbers: numbered lists to sequence writing
- first line: statement of what is to be achieved
- do not: imperatives
- read all instructions: short, clear sentences

Now she's old enough . . . :
- opening statement: return to nursing
- closing statement: if you've had a break from nursing . . . we can offer you . . .
- direct appeal to reader: what about yours? If you've had a break from nursing

- emotive language: valuable, special rewards, daunting prospect

Clues that tell you this text was written for young people:
- jokey illustration
- informal language
- content of text, dealing with parents, usually a young person's problem

Clues that tell you text was written for adults:
- type of language used (e.g. 'circumstances')
- content of text, refers to driving a car
- way in which readers are addressed: alcohol can be a positive part of your life

Practice question

Purpose of text: to persuade

Subject matter: suffering animals

Language refers to donations, suggests people are being persuaded to give
Uses emotive language such as cruelty and suffering, dedicated care
The sort of person who would read this is someone who loves animals and who would be affected by the details of the advertisement.

Understanding presentation
Check questions

No time to draw breath: presentation matches topic, because there is picture of a smoke ring, which links with topic of smoking.
Background colour is red, which suggests danger.

How would you feel?: the letter is in handwriting, you would feel someone was writing to you personally.

Practice questions

1 Three different typefaces are used.
2 Type size varies to draw attention to different parts of text.
3 Print helps to emphasise message by making key points stand out, for example: for just £2 per month.
4 Picture of children arouses readers' sympathy.
5 Picture of happy child makes you think your donation will do good. The picture of pound coins makes reader realise how little money is needed

Evaluating language
Check questions

Texts likely to use imperatives are: instructions, perhaps for a new appliance or recipes

How green are you?: makes readers question themselves, think carefully about their own behaviour

Six examples of colloquial language:
- hands up
- down the loo
- solitary spud
- yes, me too
- pretty well
- put hand on heart.

Practice questions

1 The impression is given that terrapins are dangerous creatures.
2 The headline uses the word 'peril' and the sub-heading tells readers they decimated wildlife.
3 Words and phrases used for dramatic effect are:
- plate-sized monster
- causing havoc
- gobble up insects
- wildlife will be devastated
- wily terrapins.

Comparing texts
Check questions

1 **Text A** has been written to persuade readers to take a holiday in Cyprus.
Text B has been written to inform readers about a child's life in Cyprus and also to entertain.

2 **Text A** has a picture of attractive scenery and buildings that would help to persuade the reader. It also has unusual type for the heading to attract the reader's eye.
Text B has a picture of a small boy to give the reader an idea of what the text will be about. It is written in sentences and paragraphs like an article or a story.

3 Both texts use language which makes Cyprus seem an attractive place.
For example: **Text A**
- a charmed land
- deserted beaches
- treasure trove of castles
- an enchanting land

For example: **Text B**
- lush green grass
- scented wild flowers
- sweet juicy flesh

Practice questions

1 **Text A** is about the attractions of Cyprus. It tells the reader about the sort of things they can do on holiday.
Text B is about the life of a child growing up on Cyprus. It tells the reader what life was like for a child on the island.
Both texts give the reader the impressin that Cyprus is a beautiful place.

2 Both texts present a picture of Cyprus that is very beautiful.
Both texts make the reader want to visit the island to see for themselves.

The first text persuades the reader that it is a good place for a holiday.

The second text appeals to the reader on a more personal level because he or she can identify with the reader through his or her own childhood.

Writing

Writing skills

Practice question

Correct version of paragraph:
Ever since I was little I have been interested in cycling. My first bike had extra wheels to help me balance, but I soon graduated to a BMX. I used to wear bald patches on the lawn doing my stunts.

Writing for a specific purpose

Check questions

Features of writing to persuade:
1 use of word 'you'; for example, you'll find no shortage
2 language used emotively: amazing range, staggering range
3 use of question mark, exclamation mark

YES to fireworks:
facts
• people were injured
• people killed or maimed by fireworks
opinions
• thoughtless idiots
• innocent children

NO to fireworks:
facts
• people are hurt by them
• banning fireworks would put people out of work
opinions
• an over-reaction
• an unfortunate accident

Writing to advise:
The writer has shown she understands the problems of her readers by words such as:
• 'daunting experience'
• 'you may worry'
• 'your new school is much bigger'.

Matching writing to your audience

Check questions

Examples of places where the writer has matched style to audience (children):
• use of informal language; for example, 'sort of'
• appeals to readers directly: 'you could . . .'
• uses simple language: 'pedalling was hard work'

What makes a good friend:
Vocabulary matches needs of older audience;
for example:
tactful, sympathetic, unselfish
Sentence structure is now more complicated, the text is not just written in simple sentences.
Vocabulary shows the text has been written for an older audience.

Teenage gambling:
Vocabulary suited to adult audience:
• increasingly responsible
• finance their obsession

Writing letters

Check questions

Example of informal language:
'veggie'

Shortened words:
'I'm not'
'I've noticed'

More formal vocabulary and sentence structure:
'. . . the nation has demonstrated its strong sympathy . . .'
'We should ensure that they . . .'

Writing advice sheets

Check questions

Imperatives:
• aim to . . .
• stick to . . .
• hold back
• ask yourself

Hidden advice to parents: make sure your children don't drink.

Features of writing:
A friendly tone is seen in advice such as 'walk tall and be confident' and 'ignore nasty comments'.

Writing reports

Check question

Hitting Out – features in common:
• headline
• main story in first paragraph
• uses past tense in places

Writing articles

Check question

Answers to questions about 'Wheels' article:
• article might appear in cycling magazine
• its purpose is to inform
• a keen cyclist might read this
• formal – vocabulary such as 'component', 'transform', does not use personal tone, does not refer to reader directly

Last-minute learner

Literary texts

Simon Armitage:
- Writes from personal experience.
- Uses persona to express his attitudes.
- The persona appears to be unconcerned, but this shows the poet cares deeply.
- Uses symbols to convey meaning.
- Read between the lines to understand his meaning.
- Uses unusual verse formations.

Carol Ann Duffy:
- Writes from personal experience.
- Writes about unusual happenings in her life.
- Has a realistic attitude towards love and human relationships.
- Uses symbols to convey meanings.
- Read between the lines to understand her meaning.
- Tone shifts combine a comic and a serious attitude towards life.

Ted Hughes:
- Finds the meaning of experience in the power of nature.
- Power generated by using:
  - alliteration and assonance
  - heavily stressed rhythm
  - violent imagery.
- Possesses a light touch in the humorous poems.

Poems from other cultures and different traditions:
- Divided cultures, expressed as two halves.
- Symbols are used to express both cultures (e.g. dress, place).
- Cultures change, evolve.
- Cultural change is expressed through contrasting language.
- Cultural change is expressed through languages merging.
- The poets' reactions vary between sadness and anger.

Non-fiction texts

Reading non-fiction

Tackling reading questions in an exam
Remember to:
- read the questions carefully **before** you read the text
- **underline** the key points in the question
- find **key points** in the **text** and underline them
- use **quotations** to support the points you make
- keep your quotations **short**
- match the length and detail of your questions to the number of marks awarded.

Handy hints
1 **Extracting information from two texts**
- Make sure you include roughly equal amounts of information from each text.

2 **Deciding what is *fact* and what is *opinion***
- remember: facts can be proved, they often contain **numbers**
- opinions are often introduced by *could, may, might*

3 **Following an argument**
- Look for words like *also, as a result of, in this way*, which signal the beginning of a new stage in the argument.

4 **Identifying *purpose* and *audience***
- Ask yourself: '**Why** has this text been written?' and 'What are the **clues** that tell me who it has been written for?'

5 **Understanding presentation**
- Remember to comment on the layout, headlines, illustrations and type of print.

6 **Evaluating language**
- Remember to comment on individual words and phrases.

7 **Comparing texts**
- Use these words and phrases:
  on the other hand, in contrast to, there are similarities, compared with.

Writing non-fiction

Tackling writing in the exam

Remember to:

- read the question carefully
- underline the key words in the question
- think about your purpose for writing before you begin
- make a plan to help you structure your writing
- include an introduction and a conclusion in your plan
- plan the order in which you will use your other points
- choose your vocabulary to match your audience.

Handy hints

Writing for a specific purpose

Do not start to write until you are certain of your purpose.

Matching writing to audience

Make a list of vocabulary that you will use before you begin to write.

Writing letters

Match the beginning and ending of your letter to your audience and purpose; for example, a letter to a friend has an informal beginning and ending.

Writing advice sheets

Think about using presentational devices such as headlines and subheadings to make your advice stand out clearly.

Writing reports and articles

Make a plan before you begin to make sure that your writing is very well organised. An introduction and a conclusion and four or five points is a good model.